with love

WHAT
WE WISH
WE KNEW
ABOUT BEING
QUEER AND FILIPINO
IN AMERICA

with love

WHAT WE WISH WE KNEW ABOUT BEING QUEER AND FILIPINO IN AMERICA

DUSTIN E. DOMINGO

Foreword by Grayson Villanueva

CONTRIBUTING AUTHORS

AJ Johnson

Alyssa B.V. Cahoy

Andre Zarate

AV AudVision

Dr. Arnel Calvario Ripkens

Blaine Valencia

Brandon English

Bryant de Venecia

Bunny Anne

Dianara Rivera

Dominic I.J.

elle Zulueta

Francis Joseph J. Gallego

Gabe Sagisi

Gabriella Buba

Harlee Castro Balajadia

Hazel Bondoc Carranza

Jeff Deguia

Jensen Reyes

Jessica Lustina Afable

Jobert E. Abueva

Joel Baker

Jonny Aliga

JP Rogers

Lani Fontillas

LJ Balajadia

Manny Garcia

Mara De La Rosa

Mary Sabino

Megan Dela Cruz

Dr. Michelle Fortunado-Kewin

MJ BH

Nicholas Pilapil

O. Ayes

Patrick Anthony Asence-Arradaza

Paul Jochico

P. M.

Ramon Alcantara

Rana Rosanes

Resi Ibañez

Ron Blakely

Ryan Dalusag, LCSW

Sam C. Tenorio

Sean-Joseph Takeo Kahāokalani Choo

tiano p.

Timothy A.M. Tumbokon

Toby Javier

TR Deanon

Vanessa Aczon

Warjay Naigan

Cover designed by Dustin E. Domingo

First Paperback Edition, 2024 | Paperback ISBN: 979-8-9865457-9-0

Library of Congress Control Number: 2024933486

www.KuwentoCo.com
info@kuwentoco.com
@KuwentoCo

This work is for my inner child

As well as for others who seek to be seen and heard

Especially my queer Filipino, Filipina, and Filipinx community

TABLE OF CONTENTS

Unapologetically take up space.

FOREWORD

Grayson Villanueva

Coming out can feel like you're about to jump off the edge of a cliff not knowing if there's a net at the bottom. Telling someone you're queer and not knowing what the other person will think of you is not easy, especially if it's someone you've known for a long time. I've come out to a handful of close, long-time friends with whom I feel safe. Their responses ranged from "thanks for sharing– I don't fully understand, but I'm happy you told me" to "you can tell me anything– nothing's really changed." And while I know it's a privilege to be out in the time that we live in, tolerance often disguises itself as "acceptance," and at times, it doesn't feel like enough.

However, when I came out to Dustin, something about the experience felt different. He didn't just accept me. He made me feel seen, understood, and even celebrated for my queerness. Like an *I-just-won-the-lottery* type of celebration. Dustin created a space for me to feel held and supported in a way I didn't know I needed at the time. So yeah, that's the new standard– everyone take note.

For as long as I've known Dustin, he's always been a creative collaborator and supportive friend. In all of his many artistic endeavors, whether it's singing, producing music, podcasting, screenwriting, spoken word, or poetry, one through-line in it all is his strong sense of community, support, and his superpower of empowering others. MeSearch is a podcast that he co-hosts highlighting Filipino/a/x folks succeeding in their respective industries. Dustin also narrates original short stories that often involve themes of growth and relationships. This book isn't just a collection of letters; it's a curated journey through the shared experiences of queer Filipino/a/x individuals, designed to inform, celebrate, and comfort anyone navigating their own queer journey. In the same way Dustin held a space for me to share a piece of myself, he approached this project with the same spirit: with love.

This book is a "net" for self discovery in one's queer journey and I couldn't imagine anyone other than Dustin to introduce you to all the beautiful queer Filipino/a/x folks in this book. These letters were meant to be words of empowerment and comfort for their younger selves, but they feel like they were written for any queer person looking for love and support in their own journey, or any allies looking to serve as a net for their queer loved ones.

I hope you approach this book with an open heart and open mind, ready to find pieces of your own stories from the stories of others. I hope you can find a sense of belonging, understanding, and empathy within the richness and diversity of the queer Filipino/a/x experience. And I hope you are not only celebrated, but also feel encouraged to engage in meaningful conversations, empowered to share your stories, and inspired to celebrate others in your community.

Thank you Dustin, for bringing this project to life and to the contributors for sharing your stories. I'm honored to introduce, With Love by Dr. Dustin E. Domingo.

Grayson

PREFACE

In the summer of 2023, I was let go from my full-time job in higher education after more than a decade of service. The institution had gone through multiple reorganizations and layoffs since the pandemic of 2020. During that time, I led my teams through anxiety-ridden changes and transitions. More than a few times, I found myself sitting in front of a colleague or direct report who shed tears due to the circumstances of their lives at home or work, especially throughout that first year after the Covid lockdown began. Having survived multiple employee cuts, I thought I was safe. I had years of institutional knowledge; I was an expert in my field; I built strong connections with internal and external stakeholders; and people counted on me. At the end of the day, very few people are truly indispensable in their workplace– and I was not safe from the chopping block.

·♥·♥·♥·♥·♥·

Hello, reader. If you don't know me, my name is Dustin E. Domingo. I spend a lot of time reflecting on things like purpose, passion, the universe, and existence. I'm not an astrophysicist and I'm not a religious figurehead at all. However, I often find myself wondering about how the heck we even got here. We're somehow at a point where life and technology have evolved generation after generation to allow me to type out the ideas from my brain into existence onto a page for someone else to consume. Modern-day technology allows just about anyone to imagine things into existence. We're all engineers, artists, and creators somehow. If we can imagine it; we can create it. Creation is wild. And humanity is wild. As humans, we live by a bunch of arbitrary rules that seem to make the world go 'round. We all ought to have the opportunity to imagine, right? We all ought to be able to imagine ourselves living fully in a future world that's better than the one we're in today. What do I care about? Who do I care about? What is my impact on the world? How do I live more fully? These are questions I often reflect on and I feel it is a blessing to have reached a point in my life where I can dream about my future and feel empowered to feel responsible for the trajectory of my own life.

I wasn't always like this. As a gay Filipino in the United States, I grew up without a sense of agency, without wonder, and without a feeling of control over much of what happens to me in life. I accepted that decisions were made for me. I feared that the world would view me as an *other* because I was Brown, Asian, Filipino, Gay, Effeminate, or Something Else. Even after coming out, I realized the confining nature of labels, which is why I also resonate with the umbrella term, *queer*. The beauty of the word, for me, is that it leaves room for the expanding understanding of the me I am now and of the me who always was. Furthermore, we live in a world that upholds systems that tell queer people that they shouldn't even exist. And so to be queer is inherently political and it is an act of resistance. My connection to and personal use of the word *queer* is to stand up for myself as well as to stand in solidarity with others who are oppressed and thrown to the margins by society. In the past, I strived to be loved and accepted by those who did not love and accept me. Why was I measuring my self-worth against the standards of groups that cared only to create caste systems that placed me towards the bottom because of where my family was from, because of what I looked like, and because of my sexual orientation? All of these thoughts and personal experiences led me to the decision that this book, With Love, was absolutely necessary. This book allows a community of other queer Filipinos to relate to one another and engage in meaningful discussions about lived experience, while also finding those moments of joy as we move forward in life.

.▼.♥.♥.♥.▼.

To have my career temporarily derailed for a brief moment in time became a catalyst to work on this labor of love. This is the labor that for me is worth my time and energy. I am grateful that the universe somehow opened a door for me to imagine this project and execute it with the help of others who cared deeply about making sure this book became a reality.

INTRODUCTION

Scientists believe that Earth is more than 4.5 billion years old. This chaotic floating rock in space, which we call home, has been spinning on its axis for billions of years throughout the cosmos. Now imagine for a moment, a planet is just doing whatever planets do for ages upon ages, and then all of sudden you, a little naked, vulnerable, breathing thing are born. A life that just– *POOF* –suddenly takes up space on said planet seemingly from out of nowhere. A newly birthed sentient being who also happens to be the result of generations of your ancestors who have loved, hurt, and overcome. Ancestors who have certainly felt the gamut of human emotion. Ancestors who have faced struggles and challenges that present-day generations might only imagine.

Hundreds, thousands, and millions of people in fact, were born, lived, and died in order for you, an individual, to simply exist. *POOF!* Holy crap. What a miracle indeed. What's more of a miracle is that there is only one of you. When you were born, the world had the honor of meeting you.

I truly believe that as children, we have a great awareness to know who we are and how we feel. We may not have the vocabulary to express ourselves in great detail until we practice reading, writing, or talking. Granted, language evolves as new words seemingly emerge every day. Still, we do have some innate understanding of identity and we are capable of developing a sense of self.

As we move through the various stages of life, however, we grow and we change. Sometimes this change is very clear to us. Sometimes, it's intentional. Sometimes, we're triggered into change. Sometimes, others might notice us changing before we can see it for ourselves.

What we think we're observing during this change is this: An uncomfortable evolution into someone we're not; a new person we don't know; someone far from who we were. This leads to discomfort for other people because now they're forced to do the work of meeting you and learning you all over again. You see, it's not the *change* that's hard. It's the *transition* that we can't bear. The transition is unpleasant for us and others because it involves having to relearn and reframe how we view the world. It's these paradigm shifts that rock us to our core. The social norms that we hold as inherent truths about humanity can be broken and rebuilt. Rebuilding a sense of self can take a lifetime.

For those of us lucky enough to feel more empowered and self-assured as we age, I'd like to imagine that it's not because we are moving away from who we are. Rather, I'd like to believe that those of us who begin to thrive and who begin to feel our power do so as a result of unlearning the social scripts that are taught to us growing up. Transitions are hard, but change allows us to thrive. At the end of the day, we should realize that to change is not to move *away* from who we are; it's to move *toward* who we always were. It's to become authentic to who we are despite the social scripts telling us we should be someone we're not.

This is in part why this book exists.

- To remind you that you are a miracle.

- To remind others that we, especially as queer Filipinos, can exist authentically and thrive while doing so.

- To remind us all that there is a community out there for everyone.

And when you learn to move towards your more authentic self, regardless of what our society says, there you will stand in joy, in relief, and power. One of the best gifts you can give to yourself is to be as *you* as you can be. To move towards the real *you* might be a difficult journey. This is particularly true in today's age where social scripts still overwhelmingly center heteronormative lifestyles, binary perceptions of gender and love, as well as Eurocentric standards of beauty that are simply unattainable. Especially when our ethnic heritage includes centuries of colonialism and imperialism, the intersection of our identities as queer Filipinos greatly impacts how we interact with the world around us.

Remember, our planet is 4.5 billion years old. Our giant blue marble will likely continue to spin for another several billion years before it's completely engulfed by the sun. In context, your lifespan is but an infinitesimal moment.

POOF–you're here.

POOF–you're gone.

So why not live the life you want to live? The inner peace and power that many of us crave can become a reality when we take even tiny steps toward who we always were.

Taking steps toward who we always were is a tough task. *How do we even start?* Meaningful action and change in life begin with awareness. You become more aware of your surroundings, the needs of others, as well as your own needs and desires, when you practice self-reflection. Some of the best ways to do this, I have found, are through journaling and meditation. From these practices, I have been able to get alone time with my thoughts, memories, and visions of the future. If you continue engaging in these practices, I guarantee more things will become clear; including your self-worth, your core values, and what you want out of life.

I didn't start journaling regularly until I was well into my 30s when I read *The Artist's Way* by Julia Cameron, which is a workbook for creatives who are looking for inspiration. Not only does Cameron encourage daily journaling (i.e. *morning pages*), but she also includes exercises that encourage the individual to spend time with themselves. One exercise from the book was to write a letter to my younger self. From this exercise, I began to process events in my life from an adult lens. I also was able to offer comfort and assurance to my inner child who was still with me. This powerful exercise helped heal a little bit of what I felt was broken inside of me. No wonder therapists recommend this exercise to their clients as well.

Growing up queer and Filipino in America, I felt many moments of shame and exclusion because of who I was, who I came from, where I came from, how I dressed, how I looked, how I spoke, etc. Knowing I felt a bit of healing from writing to my younger self, I wanted to encourage others who may have similar lived experiences to partake in this exercise. Moreover, in a moment in history where banning books is seen as a solution to the so-called, *problem* of queer literature, I felt it necessary to take action that would ensure stories and histories of queer communities, and especially queer Filipino communities, would not be erased.

This book, With Love, began as a project that aimed to capture the histories and perspectives of LGBTQIA+ Filipinos living in the United States using letters written by adults to their younger selves as the vessel. The writing prompt given to the community was as follows:

*Imagine you could send a letter through time to your younger self.
Write a letter to that person to inform, empower, comfort, and/or
share about your lived experiences in the United States. Keep in
mind all the sorts of messages or lessons you wish you knew that
might have helped you better navigate your world.*

As a book, With Love seeks to accomplish the following:

- Uplift and educate other queer Filipinos, especially younger generations, who are living in the United States.

- Add to the growing body of work by/for the queer and Filipino communities.

- Document the diversity of perspectives in history.

- Invite the community to participate in an exercise that will help them reflect on their personal growth, resilience, strength, and contributions to society.

Letters were collected from the community and curated into this book, With Love. Submissions that were selected to be showcased in this book included those who met the following criteria: Individuals must be Filipino; identify as members of the LGBTQIA+ community; and also currently live in or have lived a substantive number of years in the United States.

From July through October of 2023, I put out a call for submissions for this project via social media and direct outreach to various organizations. I sent several emails to undergraduate Filipino student associations across the United States, talked to friends and colleagues, and relied heavily on my community to spread the word. My initial expectation was that the vast majority, if not all of the submissions would come from Southern California because that is where I am based. I was surprised to discover that the first submissions came from Massachusetts. Before this project, I didn't even have any friends in Massachusetts. Of course, many of the submissions did come from my home state, as California has the highest population of Filipino residents in the United States. However, I was astounded by the fact that this project resonated so much that submissions came from Hawaii, Washington, Oregon, Texas, Illinois, Pennsylvania, New York, and New Jersey. I am humbled further still because submissions also came from Filipinos who have lived experiences in the United States, but wrote in from as far as Canada, the Netherlands, and Australia.

⋅♥⋅♥⋅♥⋅♥⋅♥⋅

This book is culturally significant because it allows us to proclaim to future generations that we exist. We are here and we have an extensive history in the United States, and around the globe. We deserve to have our histories preserved. The 2020 US Census reported that there were 4.4 million Filipinos living in the United States. This figure takes into consideration all Filipinos who were native-born and immigrants regardless of their citizenship status. While citizenship status is a significant part of individual Filipinos' histories in the United States, citizenship status was not one of the factors that determined who was eligible to participate in this book. For that reason, I'd like to make clear that throughout this book, I use phrases such as Filipino Americans, Filipinos in America, or Filipinos in the United States. In all instances, I intend to convey our geographic location rather than citizenship status.

The reported total population of the United States who are LGBTQIA+ will differ depending on the source and depending on when the data was collected. According to a Gallup poll (2022), the number of adults in the United States who identify as something other than heterosexual is up to 7.1 percent, which is double the amount reported in 2012. Gallup (2022) also states that more Gen Z adults identify as being part of the LGBTQIA+ community in the United States. Some might argue this uptick in reported LGBTQIA+ individuals is a cultural *trend* rather than any meaningful marker of the trajectory of society. Speaking only from personal experience, I don't identify as being queer, gay, or part of the LGBTQIA+ just because it's a trendy or fun thing to do. (Actually, let's be extremely clear, it's pretty fun over here.) Still, my point is that I feel that while it is important to explore one's gender and sexual orientation, what is *right* is truly up to the individual and is based on what feels inherent.

The language that describes the diversity of genders and sexual orientations is constantly changing to be more inclusive. The traditional perceptions of gender and sexuality, being binary and heterosexual are social constructs. *Social constructs* are ideas about the world and its inhabitants. They're ideas that we as a society accept and integrate into the ways in which we interact with each other and move about the world. Sure, if we break it down, social constructs are ideas and expectations that are real only because we as a society say they're real. So are labels fake? Yes and no. Social constructs might be ideas we're all just rolling with, but they still have massive implications on how we experience the world; who is oppressed; and who is valued.

In academia, the term *queer* is often used as an umbrella term for individuals who fall outside of the conventions of the gender binary and heterosexuality. Similarly, in this book, I use the term queer to be an all-inclusive term that captures individuals who are part of the LGBTQIA+ community. Evolving language in this context of gender also affects the Filipino community in that there are now uses of the term *Filipinx*. Additionally, other organizations in the United States and abroad may use *Pilipino, Pilipina,* or *Pilipinx*. You will find in this book, I will mostly use the term Filipino (or Filipinos). This is particularly the case when I write in reference to myself because I personally use the term Filipino in day-to-day conversations when discussing my ethnicity. I have also referenced data and academic literature that mostly uses the term, *Filipino* or *Filipinos*. I am following suit when writing about the community as a whole. Sincerely, I embrace anyone's desire to use any, some, or all of the terms: Filipino, Filipina, Filipinx, Pilipino, Pilipina, or Pilipinx. Use whatever terms resonate with you the most, and know that this may change for you over time.

· ♥ · ♥ · ♥ · ♥ · ♥ ·

With Love is about what *we* wish *we* knew about being queer and Filipino in America. I've debated heavily on how much of myself to insert into this book, but the reality is, I am part of this community. To detach myself reminds me of all those times little childhood Dustin chose to run away or to hide from who I really am. So you'll find that in each chapter, I do my own reflecting on how I relate to the experiences and stories shared by the contributing writers of With Love.

These wonderful individuals come from across the United States and beyond. The letters in this book are written by Filipinos who are of diverse genders, sexual orientations, and ages. Those featured in this book include men, women, and non-binary folks. Individuals who submitted to this project include those who have identified as lesbian, gay, bisexual, transgender, cisgender, queer, pansexual, gender fluid, demisexual, and/or sexually fluid. For ease of writing, these individuals and any others who are within the umbrella of the LGBTQIA+ community are referred to as *queer* in this book.

Furthermore, those featured in this book come from a wide range of life stages, career backgrounds, and include those with disabilities as well as those who are neurodivergent. The youngest writers were approximately 20 years old upon submission and the oldest is in their 60th decade of life. Some writers were currently enrolled in undergraduate school. Some had their doctorate degrees.

Some were employed; some were not. Some writers were single. Some were fresh out of breakups. Some were engaged or married. Some were in polyamorous relationships. Couples submitted and are separately featured in this book. Some individuals identify as queer and are currently in heteronormative presenting relationships. Siblings are featured in this book as well. I'm amazed at the broad range of life circumstances reflected in the letters you are about to read. You will be able to read about their diverse perspectives on life, love, family, and romance through their letters to their younger selves. I hope that in seeing the diversity among those showcased here, you will feel assured that there are people of all ages and backgrounds who belong to the same queer Filipino community.

Fifty queer Filipino Americans are featured in With Love and their biographies appear at the end of this book. Being that I believe wholeheartedly in the value of the exercise of writing to your younger self, this book also includes a letter I wrote to my younger self. You'll find that a number of the writers contributed multiple letters, and a total of sixty-eight individual letters were selected for publication. As I poured over each letter submitted to With Love, 10 distinct themes stood out that can be considered life lessons learned by the community, which we would like to impart upon you, the reader. Each chapter of this book represents one of these 10 life lessons that we wish we knew about being queer and Filipino in America:

1. Life is hard. Forgive yourself.

2. Beware of perfectionism, people-pleasing, and self-depletion.

3. Be critical of your relationship to religion.

4. Your parents were doing what they knew. Take it or leave it.

5. Find your chosen family.

6. Break a few rules and have fun.

7. Media has the power to change lives.

8. Finding love and being loved is a damn journey.

9. You will experience loss and heartbreak.

10. Unapologetically take up space.

Know that each and every letter submitted to With Love is dynamic and may include multiple themes and lessons expressed by the writers. However, each chapter will group 6 to 8 different letters together in a way that encapsulates one of the life lessons that have emerged. If these letters had been analyzed by another individual, perhaps the themes that stood out to them may have differed.

The culminating book, With Love, and its framework have helped me heal and make sense of my connection with the community as well as the world around me. Nevertheless, I recognize I'm operating with a lens that is uniquely my own. I presume that the majority of readers are both queer *and* Filipino. Therefore, in many instances, when I address you, the reader, it is with the presumption that you will resonate with the contributing writers in this book and directly benefit from what they've shared.

Regardless of whether you are queer, Filipino, or American, my recommendation is that you will read the letters featured in With Love multiple times to gain your own understanding of yourself and the world around you. You may resonate with many of the letters. You may disagree with the perspectives shared throughout the book. Regardless, I hope the words in With Love encourage you to reflect on your own identity. These 10 life lessons presented in this book should be a jumping-off point for you to draw your own conclusions. Perhaps this book will even inspire you to write a letter to your younger self one day and share it with me or the world.

LESSON ONE

LIFE IS HARD. FORGIVE YOURSELF.

There was a social media campaign in the 2010s– the *It Gets Better Project* (itgetsbetter.org). In many ways, this was a successful movement across the globe that brought to light the issues of violence, shame, and bullying against the queer community, as well as the suicide ideation that alas comes with the territory for many of us. *It Gets Better* is a non-profit organization that was established in 2010 and still exists today. In its infancy, the organization created and collected original content from gay adults who would convey through videos to queer youth that their lives would improve over time, despite it being filled with overwhelming depression and anxiety in the present moment.

The Trevor Project is a similar non-profit organization based in America that centers on the importance of mental health and crisis intervention services. According to a 2023 survey conducted by *The Trevor Project* (thetrevorproject.org) of LGBTQ youth across the United States, more than 40 percent of respondents have considered attempting suicide. They reported in 2022, that nearly 1 in 5 transgender and nonbinary youth have gone so far as to attempt suicide. *The Trevor Project* also found that respondents of color reported higher rates of attempted suicide than their white peers in 2022 and 2023.

At the heart of the, *It Gets Better Project* and *The Trevor Project* is the undying effort to save and celebrate future generations of queer people globally. In the same spirit, With Love exists, specifically for queer Filipinos in America as well as abroad, to help us through the challenges associated with being who we are, where we are, and when we are.

The life we've lived up to this point, and in fact, the life we're currently living, was not easy and is not easy. The United States has its own messy history of racism and socioeconomic disparities. Filipinos and the Philippines have a unique relationship with the United States, which contributes to how we navigate through our social environments. I recommend reading *Brown Skin, White Minds* by E.J.R. David (2013). For me, reading it was a seminal experience that helped me understand how the centuries of Spanish colonialism and United States imperialism of the Philippines can manifest into *colonial mentality* within Filipinos. David (2013) states that colonial mentality refers to a kind of internalized oppression wherein we Filipinos view ourselves and anything tied closely to our heritage as inferior in comparison to anything of the colonizers or oppressors. Imagine this coupled with internalized hatred taught to us by society for being queer. A double whammy of insidious mental distress. We are constantly confronted with external factors that push us into dark places. We encounter people and powers that whether intentionally or not, will oppress us, harm us, and create barriers to our hopes and dreams. This is perhaps the most obvious reality for the readers of this book, which is why we begin here.

Before you continue, I have to prepare you with a trigger warning. Some of the letters selected for this chapter include recounts of abuse and trauma that are violent and/or sexual in nature ("I'm Sorry" and "Break You"). As contributing writer, Bryant de Venecia puts it, "This deeply personal piece talks about trauma from sexual violence. The content is disturbing and may be traumatizing." If you are not up for it at this time, feel free to skip this chapter altogether or return to it at a later time when you are ready. Overall, the letters featured in this chapter ultimately include honest reflections on overcoming abuse and obstacles. This chapter includes a trigger warning, yet I feel it necessary to say that throughout this book, you will read letters that will affect you emotionally and undoubtedly will bring up painful memories of your own. This first chapter may contain content that is saddening to read, but it is a true account of events, and therefore necessary to share with our community.

My hope is that as a whole, With Love, will inspire and heal the writers of each letter as well as you, the reader. While this first chapter may include descriptions of extreme abuse, there are learning and healing moments throughout this work. You can't get to the good stuff without getting through the hard stuff. As I went through the exercise of writing my own letter to my younger self, I discovered the content of my letter explores the notion that society and the people within it have exercised their power to control me and put me into a box from which I wished only to escape. This is the first letter you will read in With Love. You will find from the others who wrote their letters about hardships and oppressors, that though life can get better, getting to that *better* place takes a lot of work. For many of us, life includes mountains that defeat us almost daily. Those frequent moments of defeat feel like failures that can't ever be forgotten. You can't help but make mistakes in life. You are human. Forgive yourself and stay kind to yourself.

SMALL WORLD BIG WORLD - DUSTIN E. DOMINGO

Dear Me,

There is no easy way to say this, but people will try to squash you. Knowingly or unknowingly, people will take multiple opportunities to kill your dreams before you have even begun to utter your deepest desires or visions for the future. They will try to shape your future before you have even begun to live your life. The cruelest people will discourage you with smiles on their faces. Even the kindest hearts try to protect you from danger, but in doing so they will stifle your growth.

It's interesting that no matter the direction you walk, you may encounter those who will keep you stagnant. You'll hear people say, "It's such a *small* world." Others will say, "It's such a *big* world out there."

The *small world camp* might tell you to be careful of what you say, or to be careful of who you love, or to be careful of how you speak and dress.

> "It's a small world. People will know you for your mistakes and judge you for who you are. What are people going to think about you!? Best to play it safe."

On the other hand, the *big world camp* might tell you that there's no point in making new friends and exploring new places; or there's no point in reaching for your dreams, or there's no point in dreaming at all.

> "It's a big world. It'll eat you alive if you try to do what you really want to do. What are people going to think about you!? Best to play it safe."

All of this is because they think they know you better than you know you. All of this is because they want to shelter you and protect you from their own traumas.

While it's true that you're still so young and every day you will learn more about yourself, remember this. You are the one who must sit in your emotions, your grief, your sadness, your anger, your joy, your ecstasy, and your liberation. The decisions you make will dictate whether you live with yourself under a dark cloud of regret or whether you will stand proudly liberated. And it's okay that you might make mistakes, but you will survive and you will learn from them. You will grow stronger every day and you will love yourself harder every day.

The fact of the matter is that you live in a world that is both big and small. Both camps can be true. Life is complex. The world we live in is complex. You will experience despair. You will experience bliss. Regardless of what camp you encounter, I encourage you to look at things differently.

It's a small world. So let's get to know the people in it. Let's build a community. Let's learn more about one another. Let's celebrate our common ground as well as our differences. What makes you unique is what will inspire and empower others.

It's a big world. So there are no limits to your potential. We are living in a world of abundance. Taking action toward the activities and passions that bring you joy can be scary, but you'll find it is oh-so fruitful.

Small world. Big world. Either way, living here can be a challenge, but it will reward you in unimaginable ways.

Please explore.

I love you so much,
Dustin

Sometimes It Gets Worse - Sam C Tenorio

Dear Sam,

You don't know it yet, but all those big feelings you're trying to push down won't go away. I know you keep trying to forget those moments as a first grader when you asked your "boyfriend" to call you Michael. Those memories won't go away either. I know why you're doing it. It's easier to try to fit in with all your straight and/or sexually uninterested fellow high schoolers (by the way, you're not doing a very good job of hiding it—those long denim carpenter shorts are like a neon sign).

It's rough right now. Unfortunately, I'm not going to tell you it gets better. I'm not going to pretend that getting older makes anything better. In some ways, it's going to get worse. There will be heartbreak. Your mom is going to cry and blame herself when you tell her you are attracted to women. You'll process that for years and hold on to a lot of resentment. You'll also get let down and let others down in the romance department. You're going to get cheated on by your first girlfriend; you're going to build your life around your grad school girlfriend who was supposed to be *the one* and she's going to hurt you (more than once); you're going to lead someone on over years because you haven't dealt with that pain properly; and then you're going to try again in earnest with someone else and have your entire sense of self taken from you. You're going to throw yourself into this woman to the detriment of your loved ones and your academic career. The abuse will be difficult, and it will reach parts of you that you didn't know could be hurt. You'll internalize everything you've been told, and you'll want to end it all. You'll seek therapy because you think you're the problem. But then one day you'll be ugly crying behind the wheel, and you'll realize it doesn't have to be like this, everything that your therapist has been trying to get you to see will come into focus. You won't even recognize it as abuse until after it's over. You'll be embarrassed by this because whiteness has blinded you and your gender has been racialized in ways you don't want to admit because as a professor of race and gender, you should have seen it coming. You're supposed to know better. But, in the end, you'll leave.

It's going to be a catalyst. That doesn't mean the abuse is going to feel worth it, but it is going to teach you something. In your 30s, you're finally going to learn that you don't have to choose other people over yourself. You're going to learn that your closest family and friends want you to be you. You're going to take the time to figure out who *you* are. For the first time you're going to let yourself be trans, not a tomboy, or kind of queer, or maybe non-binary, or a really butch lesbian (though those days are days you'll cherish forever).

You're going to meet someone. You're not going to make yourself small just to make room for her to like you. And she's going to like you. Heck, she's going to love you. She's going to let you grow and be messy and work out who you are and who you can be. It's going to help that she has a little brother who's trans. You're going to feel comforted by the fact that you don't have to explain yourself every day. You're going to learn how to navigate this world as a queer couple that doesn't hide, together. She's going to visit the Philippines with you and she's going to love it. She's going to leave her job so she can be your primary caregiver when you have top surgery. When you're lying awake in your recliner one night because the pain is too much, you're going to realize that you want to be with this person forever. You're going to feel crazy because you haven't even been together for a year. You're going to propose and she's going to say yes. You're going to buy a house and move across the country together. You're going to get married.

Your family is going to embrace everything that you are in all your complexity and contradiction. Your siblings are going to have your back every step of the way. Mom and Dad are going to use your he/him pronouns (they're also going to mess those up, a lot), they will love your wife like a daughter, and barely bat an eye when you tell them you've started T. You're going to have friends who are family and they're going to cheer you on from all their distant corners of the country.

And one day you're going to be writing this letter to your younger self and realize all the things you thought you'd never have are right here. I'm sorry life feels so untenable right now. I'm sorry that I am not going to make the best decisions to take care of you. I'm sorry that we're going to make ourselves so small that we almost disappear. Please know that over the next 20 years, I will be learning how to love us and working through the mistakes that hurt you even as I'm making new ones. I hope you'll forgive me. Don't quit. I promise life will give you more than it takes away.

Love,
Sam

I'M SORRY - BRYANT DE VENECIA

Trigger warning: This deeply personal piece talks about trauma from sexual violence. The content is disturbing and may be traumatizing.

My love,

There was a time when I used to write letters to my future self.

Before I knew about manifestations and dreams, I was already writing to the Bryant who would have achieved it all. There was a time when I welcomed the pain and the hope simultaneously, allowing them to flood me until the rushing currents became louder than my crying. I still remember all the letters you wrote to me. I realize now that I never wrote back.

I remember when you were 6, learning to draw the human anatomy by copying the Sailor Moon characters from your sister's notebook much to Dad's annoyance. Before you identified as an immigrant, a cis gay man, a settler, a changemaker, or anything else, you were first an artist.

I remember the 9-year-old Bryant, who would hitch on the back of a tricycle to go to the bakery just to see his girlfriend, Rachel. That time when we were 11, amid our parents' violence, we prayed to God for the mercy of death. The 16-year-old who fell in love with a boy for the very first time and hated everything about himself for feeling something that was forbidden. Our 18-year-old self, stripped naked at the U.S. embassy in Manila, every crevice of my body checked to assess if I was worthy of an American visa. I will always remember every version of you, of us.

The life we live is not easy. But I can say as I write this, between your vantage point and mine, it gets better.

My love, you have inherited a resilience that came with an apology. You often wondered why your mother's love took the form of a sorry—a butterfly perched on a petal, remorseful that the flutters it took to safety created tornadoes elsewhere. When only two generations separate your birth from the war, survival is of utmost importance. In our family, 'I'm sorry' means 'I love you'.

Because of this, you will grow up associating love with shame. Ashamed of your frailty, of your tendency to present yourself to the world with gentleness and grace. Embarrassed by your emotions and sensitivity, the way you navigated every space with hesitation because a tear would fall before you could prove to the world that you are capable of being strong, powerful, and masculine. Ashamed of your past that carries darkness, you walk with a façade of humor so people will not start asking questions. I still see you.

When I moved to Hawaii, I thought the darkness would not follow. But it took up more space in my suitcase than the three pairs of shirts and two pairs of pants I brought with me to start a new life. It will be years before I will realize that your pain was here to stay. I still get to relive parts of this darkness every day. Each night, I get to revisit the old house, the old streets, the bloodstained window, and the shattered door, the mundane spaces where parts of you were taken away. They are always vivid in my dreams.

There was a time when our body was yours. You were proud of how fast you ran, of your ability to climb anything, of your light and airy voice that resonated through the church halls. You were the smart and creative child who filled up his time reading and sketching. There was a time when your agency was yours alone; you used it to explore every inch of your skin and test every joint's flexibility. Your body was *yours*.

My love, this body will be tainted by desires that your innocent mind will struggle to understand. Masked as affection feeding your longing, they will take more than what they can give. Regrettably, it will happen again and again. I want you to understand that none of that was your fault. The empty rooms and locked doors were your sanctuary from the chaotic world outside. The souls who laid siege to your made-up fort and their plundering of your innocence do not define who you are. You are only a child.

You asked in one of your letters to me if I have any regrets. Yes, my love, I have many.

I wish I held your hand when you were 5 and told you, "Don't go." Don't follow him. Don't listen to him when he says that is how it's done. I wish I could explain that the thrill of being wanted is not worth the years of agony and dissonance that will haunt our nightmares and drive our wanting. I regret not running away at 22 after he said, "Stay for a little bit." I'm sorry that I drank too much in Castro at 24; for not speaking up to my friends as they betrayed me, as they watched without saying anything. I apologize that even at 26, I failed to stand my ground and believe my own words. When I said 'no', he still consumed me because I loved him. They all lied, my love. Yours was the only truth.

I still weep over the times when I did not fight for you. I apologize for not unleashing the anger. You will discover as time goes by that your tiny body will grow into one that is capable of destruction. You will train this body to be strong and to tolerate more pain, but you'll soon realize that no form of self-defense will heal you from your shame. I want you to know, my love, you can let this shame go. In those moments of threat, *your* stillness is the act that saved *me*.

I am 30 now. I spent the last decade healing. Endless hours crying at my therapist's office, struggling to reconcile the shame and the forgiveness. But along the way, I met people who showed me the kind of love that doesn't require the sacrifice of our body. I found our voice again and our love for storytelling. I want you to know that from our pain bloomed a heart that is capable of holding so much love. I'm surrounded by families who chose me and spaces that always keep me safe. The in-betweens are filled with laughter, gentleness, and peace.

I have learned that there will never be answers as to why we had to go through all those experiences, but it doesn't mean that I cannot honor you by moving forward. The flutters that took you to safety did not unleash tornadoes—they created the winds that moved my waves.

We are now an uncle to a 2-year-old boy and another baby girl is coming. Sometimes, I look at Elijah and I remember you. He got your sense of humor and your energy. But he gets to live in a world that is safer and filled with love. The resilience they'll inherit will come with tenderness and strength, in place of an apology. The cycle of violence ends with me.

My only advice for you to survive the coming years is to honor your truth. You are enough as you are. Remember that as much as you have inherited resilience, you've also received joy, hope, will, and queerness. In you is the full spectrum of your ancestors' humanity. When the world questions your worth, you know the truth.

My love, I am here now. I'm late but I got you now. You didn't deserve everything that you went through but it's all over. It's safe now, you can come out. I hope you can be proud of me for being strong as I am proud of you for not giving up.

I'm sorry,
Bryant

HuMAN, You ARE - RYAN DALUSAG LCSW

Ryan (14) –

It's 2003, right? You just turned 14. I know it's been a tough year; some call the teenage years the toughest.

Your parents are separating/divorcing, you loved and lost your first relationship with a girl, you're struggling in school academically and socially, and you feel lost and confused. It feels like everything is crumbling beneath your feet.

But please don't give up. I know you've wanted to give up, to end it all. To just sleep, forever. The things happening in your life aren't your fault though. There are things we just can't always control.

Life is hard and confusing, maybe it feels even hopeless at times. But trust, things have and will get better. In so many different ways, the challenges lead to some of the most amazing moments.

The biggest thing I think I've learned, or am still continuing to learn...is that everyone is human, is fallible, and makes mistakes. Including you. And as humans, we can work towards learning, growing, and being better.

Your parents had their pasts and made mistakes. They came to this country from the Philippines to start anew, to live and create lives for themselves, for you and your siblings. They weren't perfect. Far from it. Their love was flawed. But they did their best in their own ways. They cared, maybe not always in the way we wanted or needed. Even up through the divorce, and after, they still love you. No matter how distant that love may feel. It's okay to forgive them.

You have some amazing friends who truly do care. Even if you feel alone, their presence is there. Learn to lean on them more. And you'll make many more friends who will come and go. Just know that you can be your true, vulnerable self. You're allowed to be open about your thoughts and emotions. There are people who genuinely care and are willing to help if you allow them to. They will love you unconditionally.

You are allowed to love who you want to love. I know you're scared, confused even. You didn't mean to hold back, but your insecurities get the best of you. You'll make mistakes, you'll get hurt, you'll even hurt people. But I hope you can learn to love more wholeheartedly. Give your all, it's so much more rewarding when you can show up as your authentic self, even if it hurts. I regret holding back, but once you learn to love yourself, allow yourself to pour that love out to others.

I know. It's been hard. You don't fully know who you are, what you want, where you want to go in life. You're confused about your sexuality, your identity, your passions. But don't let fear hold you back. Embrace the unknown and uncertainty more; you don't have to control it all. You don't have to be perfect enough, "white" enough, to always try to fit in. You can stand out; embrace the brownness of your skin; the smell of your culture's food; being nerdy and awkwardly passionate about the things you enjoy. Learning about and understanding Filipino culture was one of the most transformative experiences of my life. Find your passions, and explore different careers. You can do anything. Don't limit your options. Explore your sexuality. Don't hold back and don't hyperfocus on one aspect of it. You are allowed to break out of the mold, to be adventurous, to experiment, and to make mistakes.

You will succeed. You will fail. But don't completely give up. I know there are dark moments, moments when you find yourself in a hole that feels so consuming. But there are also so many beautiful and hopeful moments that you'll miss if you stop now. Laugh, cry, move, connect. You are human. The best part of being human is we can change.

Mahal na kita (I love you and you are loved),
Ryan (34)

BREAK YOU - FRANCIS JOSEPH J. GALLEGO

Fuck Francis,

It is true, the rape will break you into so many fucking pieces, but it will not destroy you.

It will trigger every fucking wound that you have tried to cover and hide, but it will force you to heal in ways because it has ripped you open.

There will be so much fucking loss, so much grief, so much pain; but there will be healing. Sit in the anger, sit in the humility, sit in the pain. Don't push it away, but don't let the temporary feelings make you make permanent decisions. You will hurt people, but you will help people. You are human. Read that again: *You are human.*

There will continue to be days in which you feel like you go back, and you are 5 or 19, or 29 again; but remember that sorrow, grief, and reflection have given you so much grace.

You deserve healthy love. Soak in that; healthy love. You are not your trauma. You are not your mom and her trauma.

Make your boundaries; find your beauty. Forgive yourself and self-soothe yourself; so you don't find your demons in the places that are supposed to be healing.

You don't need to beg for love; because you are love; in all its rawness and ugliness and healing glory.

Sit with it.

                                                                    Francis

It's Not Easy Being Green – Patrick Anthony Asence-Arradaza

To the Green Me,

So much of what I want to impart to you will change the way you view the world. But as much as I want to protect you and give you all the tools you need to live the best life you deserve, it wouldn't be worth living if you had everything handed to you. In fact my beautiful boy, you've had to earn so much of what you had and sacrifice pieces of you that you may find precious now but only to realize they are only small pieces of the road you built to the person you are today.

I want you to live your life on your own terms and define what it is to live life. Nothing is more true than this fact. The following is what it means to live. To be brave beyond an abyss you feel you cannot escape. To find love that envelops you and holds you close at your most vulnerable. To authentically and proudly live so loud that your being reverberates through those whom you touch with your presence. To know how valuable time is and that time wasted is time forever gone. To realize that the unicorns of your life will always be unicorns etched in fantasy and the what-ifs. To find people who will guide you with their adoration and love for you. To believe in yourself above everyone's perception and expectation of you because your life will forever be like the river of your existence: perpetually changing, flowing, and moving.

I cannot give you the blueprint that you wish you'd want from me. It is in your choices, stories yet to be told, and lessons yet to be learned, that will replenish your life's ink of your blueprint.

One wish I have for you is to always lead with mind and heart. Moreso, your big heart with your curious mind in tow. I promise you that the road ahead will thank you for keeping these two frenemies together.

And one more thing before I send you off to an adventure of a lifetime, I love you, Patrick. I am proud of you. You are wonderful and amazing. You are a warrior. You are resilient. You are one of a kind.

Truly Yours,
Your Tempered Self

I Promise - AJ Johnson

Dear little AJ,

I know you learned to stay small and quiet and convenient when being anything else meant you ended up punished or abandoned. I understand that when others were unable to reflect your glory back to you, why you talked yourself out of ever going to them again to save yourself from the hurt and disappointment.

Thank you for doing all you could do to protect yourself from the overwhelming grief and anger, even if it meant creating lies about what you were worthy of.

Thank you for surviving the only ways you knew how, my sweet and salty little love.

It was often messy.
Lonely.
Bloody.
Tearful.
And it was gritty, desperate, resilient, and brave.

And I will no longer allow myself or anyone else to shame you for it.

There's nothing to forgive you for. You didn't know what you didn't know. You couldn't do what you were never taught. You knew no other way besides what you learned. You made it through until today, even though there were times you almost didn't.

And now I've learned new ways.
To survive.
To live.

You can let go of the things that once protected you from feeling so hurt, helpless, and unworthy. I promise.

It's scary. You didn't know how to hold those feelings without being submerged in them. So you found and invented ways to keep them at bay, to keep yourself safe from them and that's okay.

But you don't have to continue to do those things. Okay? my precious little stinker, I promise.

I promise that there will come a time when the people in your life will not experience your thoughts, feelings, wants, and needs as inconveniences, but as invitations to know you more intimately.

I promise that the right people will sit with you through the suck of conflict and feel their feelings without treating you as if your humanity is a nuisance.

They will offer you compassion instead.

And it will break your heart open to be held with such tenderness and grace...and you will not be able to keep the pain and shame that you've kept buried from trickling down your face...and you will be awed at what it is to be loved.

I promise,
AJ

LESSON TWO

Beware of perfectionism, people-pleasing and self-depletion.

I was absolutely terrified to write this chapter.

Am I doing this right? Am I doing justice to the folks who have graciously given their time and energy toward contributing a piece of their personal story to the world?

I remind myself that the process of putting this book together includes holding with care, the private and tender moments documented by members of our community. This is a big responsibility and I would be lying if I told you I stayed strong throughout this entire process.

I just want to do right by the contributing writers. I want to do right by you, the reader. I want to do right by everyone.

I'm certain this is a familiar feeling to many of you reading this.

You cannot please everyone. There will unquestionably be some readers who might not resonate with any of the content in this book. They may wholeheartedly disagree with my assessments or they may dislike my writing style or maybe they dislike that this project exists at all. As a human being, it is impossible to be everything to everyone. Yet as a queer Filipino, I cannot help but try. I cannot help but over extend and overexert myself to appease others and to feel like I am capable of meeting everyone's expectations, despite my perceived shortcomings or insecurities.

Even now as I write this, I am doing so while thinking of the many projects, persons, and organizations to which I have (over)committed myself. While writing for With Love and supporting and engaging other queer Filipinos who were interested in contributing their letters to this book, I was writing for other projects, taking an acting class, producing and editing a podcast (surprise I have a podcast, follow @mesearchpodcast), rehearsing and performing with multiple a cappella groups (surprise I'm a Filipino who likes to sing), and working for multiple institutions of higher education for more than 40 hours a week. I feel like while doing all of this to appease others and/or to collect accolades, I often find my physical and mental health wavering; and my personal relationships suffering. Why am I doing this to myself?

Multiple people have commented on how it is possible or impossible to do absolutely everything I've set out to do. Frankly, I'm perpetually tired, anxious, and on the brink of burnout. That's not a badge of honor; it's something I am working on. I am grateful for my friends who bring me down to Earth and encouraged me to exercise my boundaries, extend my timelines, and forgive myself when things don't go precisely the way I imagined.

What comes to mind is *Brown and Gay in LA*, a book written by Filipino scholar, Dr. Anthony Ocampo, about the lives and perspectives of gay Filipino and Latino men in southern California. It's from his book I learned about the term, *academic covering*. In his book, Ocampo (2023) states that it refers to a phenomenon found amongst queer Filipino (and Latino) youth wherein they put in the tremendous work to excel academically in school to avoid disappointing their families for being queer. The key sentiment here is that many queer Filipinos feel it necessary to excel, hustle, and maintain a persona of perfection so that others can see that they have succeeded *despite* being queer; as though being queer in itself prevents anyone from developing any type of skill or talent.

This is where I let out the heaviest sigh one can muster. *sigh*

Look at me, a queer academic, doing what queer academics do. Researching and writing in my *free time*.

Fun fact, the audiobook for *Brown and Gay in LA* is voiced by Grayson Villanueva who is a queer Filipino American actor, vocal artist, music producer, and a dear friend, who I'm honored to say also wrote the foreword for With Love. Grayson is a self-proclaimed *multipotentialite*, which refers to an individual who pursues multiple creative and professional passions concurrently. Part of me feels like perhaps this is also a descriptor that applies to me as I say "yes" to everything but a good night's rest. Truthfully, I find myself depleted after long stretches of over-committing and over-performing.

To be completely transparent, my initial goal for With Love was to collect letters, analyze them, and write this book within 5 months. How hard could it be? I found myself disappointed in my progress both times I extended my timeline. Things work out the way they're meant to work out. And I'm glad that this work and the stories it contains are now in the hands of our peers, elders, and future generations.

This is quite something to be proud of, but I find myself in need of screaming from the highest peak that I deserve to rest. We deserve rest. You deserve rest. In reading many of the letters submitted to With Love, I found myself in awe of *who* contributed. I am humbled by the individuals who contributed to this project, many of whom I look up to and whose contributions to the community I wholeheartedly respect. The letters chosen for this specific chapter do an excellent job of capturing this common theme amongst queer Filipino Americans.

We enter this world feeling less than, as though we are starting at a deficit. So, to overcompensate, we develop multiple masks so to speak, to appease multiple groups. We can easily lose ourselves in the process. We give so much of ourselves to our communities of practice to the point where our own lights fade out. We give our energy to others and sacrifice our well-being, only to be praised for our willingness to suffer through it for the greater good.

Those whose letters are featured in this chapter reflect on the years they've strived for perfection; the labor they've exerted because they have felt like they needed to work harder to earn love and respect; the hesitance to ask for help; and at the end of the day, the call for recognition that we are enough as we are.

This is where I remind myself to breathe.

As many wise folks say, we are not human *doings*; we are human *beings*.

PEANUT - MANNY GARCIA

Dear Peanut,

That's what they call you because your name sounds like the Tagalog word for the legume. I always thought of it as simply cute and endearing – your sisters still call you Peanut Brother to this day – but the more I think of the word/our nickname, the more the meaning of it shifts.

You're going to spend much of your life in a shell, sweet Peanut. Many shells, even. And it's going to start from a young age. You'll start out sensitive and shy. You won't like smiling with your teeth because you think you'll look silly. You'll want to talk to other kids, but will be afraid of what they think of you. You'll be scared of saying the wrong things, so oftentimes you won't say anything at all. This will change, dear boy. You'll find your voice; it'll just take you a while. Don't rush it because once you do find it–once you crack open that shell – oh, how powerful your voice will be.

In thinking about these shells, Peanut, I hesitate to tell you to cast them aside altogether. You see, shells are there to protect. They stop the creatures of the world from trying to eat us. They shield us so we don't get hurt when we fall. They shelter us from the rain when it storms. But shells can also inhibit. They can stop us from growing with their hard walls. They hide our true selves so no one can see how amazing we are inside. They can be a dark confine that prevents us from seeing the sky, the light, and the beauty in the world around us. How can I tell you to leave your shell when I know how much protection it's given you? Perhaps I'll tell you, and then you can decide.

At 5, you'll learn that you even have a shell, and that it's important for it to be beautiful, shiny, and perfect all the time. You'll get your first lesson in people-pleasing – you won't know that's what it is, but it'll change the trajectory of your life. Mom and Dad will give you a new toy and it will become your favorite. You'll spend hours and hours with it every day until they tell you to give it to another kid, because it'll make him happier; and making other people happy is supposed to make you happy. You're too young to understand at 5, but you'll wipe away the tears away, separate with your favorite toy, and be told to smile as you do it. Why the other boy's happiness was more important than your own is something you'll never know, but this moment will define you. You'll be sad and smile. You'll be angry and smile. You'll be jealous and smile. You'll feel like giving up, and still, you'll smile. This smile – this perfect, curated facade – will be your first shell, Peanut. You'll build it and build it and build it until you don't even realize it's a shell anymore, that it's just part of you. You'll even smile and be unsure if you're smiling out of joy, or just smiling because it's the only thing you know how to do. If there's any shell you break out of, let it be this one. This shell just gets harder over time.

At 8, you'll know you're different from the other boys. You'll already have seen the bin of Barbies in Kindergarten, so colorful and fun with all their accessories, but you'll watch as the one boy who plays with them gets made fun of. You'll tell yourself you shouldn't play with them either. Within the safety of your bedroom, though, you'll tie a towel around your head and pretend it's long hair. You'll wrap a second towel around your body and imagine a gown. You'll twirl and prance and flounce around the room, taking note of how your hair swings to one side of your face, and how the fabric of your gown drapes over your shoulder. How I wish you kept dancing, Peanut. You'll be told it's wrong not because anyone caught you, but because one day, you'll be riding with your Tito in the car and he'll tell you to uncross your legs. "Don't sit like that," he'll spit out with disgust. "That's how girls sit. You're not a girl, right?" Until you're a teenager, you won't allow yourself to sit with crossed legs again. This is a shell I want to tell you to destroy, but I hesitate. This is a shell that camouflaged us when we were amongst predators; when the machismo of our Filipino culture attacked the femininity born within us; when we needed to put on a mask to survive. But the shell that protected us also destroyed us. Building this shell became your closet, one that you struggled to come out of – one that you'll still struggle with even when you're older.

At 12, you'll get followed home from school. It'll happen a lot over the winter. Three boys from the grade above you will follow you almost to your door. They'll yell things at you, but you won't remember what they are. You'll try and shut them out by pulling your hood up and lacing it tight, dampening the words and slurs, and the literal sticks and stones. They'll pelt you with ice blocks they picked up from the street and rocks disguised as powdery snowballs. One day they'll catch you and they'll beat you. They'll shove your face into the ground, pin you down, hit you, and laugh at you. You won't know why – maybe it's because you put your hand on your hip sometimes, or talk to the girls more than the boys; or maybe because your skin is brown, or because your eyes are shaped differently than theirs. Maybe they smelled the *chicken adobo* or *bistek* in your lunch and felt that it should've been a ham sandwich. The next shell you'll build will be here – now, not just to hide the rainbow within your heart, Peanut, but also the brownness, the *kayumanggi*, of your skin. You'll ask Mom for a Lunchable instead of *adobo*. You'll mimic vowels and syllables to make sure everyone knows you're from Chicago, and not Manila, even though you were born here. You'll get called a Twinkie and "the whitest Asian I know," and you'll even feel flattered if people think that you're only half-Filipino. You'll start dismantling this shell soon, but feeling the need to chameleon yourself won't go. You can let go of this shell, Peanut. It's okay. In a couple of decades, these people will be lining down the block to eat at our restaurants, go to our festivals, and ube is going to be a thing. Like, a really big thing.

At 17, your shell will break for the first time. Your entire academic career until this point will be flawless (Bs weren't allowed in our family); you'll be taught to be the best at everything and to do it all with a smile on your face. This immense and impossible pressure will feel like the world is on your shoulders, and no one was meant to carry the weight of the world. Your grades will slip. You'll sit on the bathroom floor for hours staring at your hollow reflection until you become a blur. Your friends will notice that something is off. Life will feel impossible, Peanut. I'm so sorry that you'll go through this because none of it is your fault. It's not even entirely Mom and Dad's fault. The immigrant mentality of succeeding in white America is what drives this generational behavior. The exceptionalism you've fallen into is a queer trauma response – that maybe if you're better than the bullies, they won't bully you. This is why I struggle to tell you what to do with the shell - the multitudes of shells - that you've built over time. You spent your entire childhood constructing your shell, fortifying it, using it to achieve great things, and then once you hit the cusp of adulthood, it imploded.

At 36, I still struggle with what to do. And maybe there isn't an answer, little legume. Maybe it's not about smashing your shell or solidifying it; maybe it's about knowing when to strap on the armor, and when to lay it down. I want you to be safe and protected, but I don't want you to harden so much that you've lost yourself. When you spend so much time pretending, so much time making everything perfect, you begin to lose your grip on what's real and what's just an empty shell. I don't have it figured out just yet, but I'm trying. I'm working on it for you and us. I love you, dear Peanut. You'll be fine. It will take you some time to get there, but you will be. Just promise me you'll come out of your shell every now and then; not just so that the world can see the beautiful, sparkly, silly, smart, brave, and compassionate boy you are...so that *you* can.

With Love,
Me

BABY GIRL - MEGAN DELA CRUZ

To younger me,

How closely I want to hold you
To finally give you the unconditional love that has eluded us
Feeling maternal and paternal love and protection
Forever ripped from our childhood
Creating a young woman so lost
So out of touch with reality and her body
That she blindly went through life, thinking "This must be love"
Settling for cis-het romances

We eventually ran our body into the ground
After a decade of organizing as a student,
Advocating as a professional,
Attempting to "stop AAPI hate"
None of the *work* we did felt fulfilling enough
To justify the trauma I endured from "pushing through"
As I constantly sat on death's porch

Year after year, attempting to find some stability
Overwhelmed with breaking generational wounds
We will still be too political and too passionate
Too sensitive, too left, too radical
To fit into the capitalist Filipino nuclear family dream
Maybe try just working on you
A dear friend once told me

A gentle call back to my body
I have never felt more present in my life
That's when I realized I *hated* you, my younger self
And I understand why you felt so scared to show up
With all the cruel and mean things I would say
About our body, our forgetful and chaotic mind
It wasn't easy acknowledging how much I berated you
Completely shit on anything you enjoyed because you were bad
Nothing was ever good enough for me

My disability and my queerness bubbled up to the surface
I was 25 when I started to acknowledge new aspects of my identity
Because I began questioning every relationship
Realizing I have no idea what it means
To be romantically *intimate* with someone else

Only then I was able to meet you, younger Megs
At 27 years old, I left everything I had built behind
It was so fucking uncomfortable
Treating myself with kindness
Treating *us* with patience and love
For the first time

At 28 we finally don't feel like dying every day
We have friends and family who love us too
Anxiety doesn't rule our life anymore
But the most shocking thing is
I love you

Don't let this world harden you, baby girl
I know it hurts so much
Because we desperately want to be loved
To finally have that white picket fence
With a boyfriend and a picket fence to match
But, baby, we deserve so much better
Someone who will cherish our body
Someone who will hold our insecurities without judgment
And we will not settle for anything less

I love the way we love
The way we're able to pick ourselves up
Through all the tragedy we've faced in our life
Alongside a community of beautiful souls
That celebrates your disability and queerness
Along with our rich Pinay ancestry
We are a vital part of our community
Where love doesn't come at the cost of labor

Keep shining, babes.

With Love,
Ate Megs

Barely Out of Third Grade - Toby Javier

Dearest Toby,

Hi. It's me; you, but in your late 30's. I imagine you're so confused with life right now. Hey, I don't blame you. You're in Manila. A magical place of friendship and connection. At the same time, the smallness of it leads those important around you to be more concerned about what people think of you above all else.

I know you're trying to be perfect right now. You're barely out of third grade and already the mediator of a chaotic family. The fights are unbearable and I'm sorry you have to put yourself in the middle - even at times getting hurt yourself, but I know that it hurts more inside than anything else.

Amidst all this, you're trying to be perfect in school. You come home and feel like a failure with anything below 90%. You're more scared of the rage and disappointment that awaits you if you don't reach this. Honestly, it's ok - in the long run, those grades and honors don't mean much.

One day you'll find a reprieve. You think everything is finally settling and you've found peace and the right family dynamic with new figures that enter your life who you can trust. You will confuse the trust and affection for love, and find comfort in it. You carry the guilt of this for a long time. I want to remind you as I remind myself now: You were a child. None of what happened was ever your fault. You were not the adult in the situation. As an adult now I understand more and more that you are not to blame - you were never to blame. This should have never happened and been done to you.

Your guiding light is your passion for the arts and trust me; it will take you a very long way. You end up in Los Angeles like you always wanted. Can you believe that? Hang in there until you get to LA because this is the place where you get a chance to start again and begin to heal. You take better care of yourself and therapy will change your life.

You will be guarded because of all that's happened. Times can be lonely, but at times you look at your life and realize how much love there is with all the experiences, family, and friends. Your work will take you to work on Hollywood sets, historic stages, and dream concert halls - remember to take all the moments in. You worked hard for it and you belong there.

I want you to love who you are because a part of you always feels like being gay is so wrong. I'm so sorry that you feel that and at times still feel that. We can work on this together. How I wish this was something we could fix instantly, but that's not how it works. I want you to know you are a good person. Maybe all of this happened because you can be the voice for those struggling to accept themselves. You can be the voice for those who are not the loudest in the room. You can be the voice for the ones who are sensitive and putting themselves together from being broken. You are so much stronger than you think and I am proud of you.

Love always,
Toby

It's Not Your Fault - AJ Johnson

My precious AJ,

I am so sorry this world is so lonely for you, that it so often feels like you've missed out on something that everyone else inherently understands.

I'm so sorry that you have felt different and weird and separate...and that you've come to believe that the chasm between you and others has grown too wide to bridge.

It's not your fault.

At 7 when you didn't play, you counted the times you could walk on the wooden beams that surrounded the playground before you could fall off...

At 10 when you stayed in to do extra math at recess...

At 11 when the universe offered you the saving grace of competitive sport to pour your time into as a distraction...

It's not your fault.

I can feel your deeply held pain, so excruciating, so soul-destroying, that you developed all kinds of ways to survive it. The isolation and hyper-independence were inevitable. So too were the people pleasing and the caretaking.

I can imagine the relief that was felt when you started to be able to figure out what people wanted from you and grasped onto that like a life raft.

And why you spent so much of your life in relationships with people who told you clearly what they wanted despite their inability to give.

The denial of your own wants and needs, as offerings to try and appease anyone that offered you a friendship that you couldn't understand.

The perfectionism and overachieving and body-focused obsessions, because even if you couldn't create intimacy with others, you learned that you could earn admiration and it would sometimes, almost feel like enough.

From your environment, you were only taught how to react to others, not to act with any agency or of your own volition. There was no reciprocal sharing of thoughts, feelings, or inner worlds. There was just surviving.

I know there are layers and layers to your grief. There will come a time when you can share this hurt with me so I can help you bear it.

So that you can heal.

So that I can tell you that the chasm is not too wide...

That you will grow up and interacting won't always be as terrifying as it once was...

That you will learn the things you need to to be able to create conscious, intimate relationships...

That you will find people who can see you and love you for who you are, not because you anticipate and provide what they want...

That the loneliness was never your fault but a reflection of the limitations of the people around you...

And that you are, and always have been worthy of a full life of healthy connections.

With all my love,
Big AJ

On Paths Leading To Where We Are - Dominic I.J.

Dear Fresh Out of High School Me,

Strap in. Keep resilient. Recognize your individual journey before, now, and ahead. You are about to transition into a significant stage: Graduating high school. Adding onto this important stage, you are feeling the pressure as the eldest child from an immigrant family, the guinea pig, the role model for your siblings. Now adding onto *this*, you are constrained by your gay identity within a military, immigrant, and heavily Catholic family. You've grown up with phrases from parents and extended family with memories of a homeland that they have left. Phrases like "You are here in this *great land of opportunity*", "make the most of the *opportunities* that you have", and *"Do things right the first time* or don't do it at all." But with this heavy expectation to do your own family right, how do you keep up with handling your own baggage as well?

It *is* a lot on your plate. You may feel that peers surrounding you seem to have it all put together. They seem to know where they are going ahead toward their career goals, toward their next life stage, and beyond. But not everyone in your social circle or high school class can relate to your individual journey, so *take a breath*. While these pressures of being the oldest child and being the gay child are overwhelming, they are all integral in shaping the path toward where *we* are now. Take ownership of these nuanced experiences. Take control of your narrative to help define your next step and decision.

I wish I had better control of my narrative after high school and during college. You may feel gnawing pressure to succeed to demonstrate something for yourself. To succeed *in spite of you being gay*. As if the small shame or disappointment you may currently perceive with your queerness is something that *sets you back*. You may resort to the pre-medicine route in university at the urging of your family, parents, and peers. There may be a concerned voice in the back of your mind that keeps whispering, "They may not approve of you being gay, but *at least you are a doctor.*" As I am writing that, I have to pause from the cringe because that *is* a problematic statement to believe and that *is* one of the many thoughts that you have had to confront and shut down later in life. But know that the fact that I *am* cringing means that significant growth and progress *has been made* towards coming to terms with your gay identity.

Unbeknownst to them, this career path takes more and more energy away from other important hurdles such as reconciling with your gay identity and therefore becoming your most authentic self. The dissonance of accepting your identity and the escalating stress of "academic success" may eventually lead to a constant feedback loop that further entrenches your feelings of debilitating anxiety, burnout, and defeat. But that *does not mean that your story is over.*

The first step was seeking community and coming to terms with its history. I've sat present and attentive as friends and loved ones shared their own experiences grappling with their queer identity. I've taken to heart the deep conversations and resonating stories from fellow Filipino mentors who have gone through similar pains and obstacles pursuing college and their future careers. I've learned more about the historical past of not only our LGBTQIA+ community but also the Filipino experience in America. All this is to get closer to better *know myself in the past, present and future*–from understanding my previous struggles growing up to navigating my future path as a queer Filipino.

I now believe that seeking satisfaction and happiness later in life is not tied to a singular job, position, or action. It is from pursuing our passions, what we enjoy, and our interests that will constantly evolve and change. *Happiness will just be a byproduct you come across along the way.* Through this manner, your feelings of success *and content* are in large part *because* you've embraced your gay identity while engaging with your queer and allied community, *and not in spite of it.*

Take the time to think introspectively about your mental health, your gay identity, your career goals, and your life goals. The path ahead may not seem clear-cut, but one of the hardest lessons to appreciate is that *nothing is ever straightforward.* It takes a level of maturity to appreciate these small nuances. *There is no traditional path to your career or personal life.* You have been raised with a narrative of *an* American Dream that (at the time) did not consider the unique life experiences of people of color, first-generational families, or queer individuals. If there is no singular traditional path, then there is no singular American Dream to confine the intricate subtleties of one's identities nor the collective histories of whole communities. Multiple Dreams *can exist* simultaneously when you dedicate the time and effort to carve out those winding roads for not only yourself, but for your community now and in the future. *So, embrace and take ownership of the non-traditional and diverse narrative that you offer.* I promise it will all be worth it. Besides, there's some fun to be had with the path less traveled.

With gratitude,
Dominic

ENOUGH - VANESSA ACZON

Dear Love,

It is I/You, your 2023 self. So, I totally *Back to the Futured* this letter. Yes, it is quite odd, or possibly kismet that this time-traveling message has met you on this very day. The day that Mom discovered that your fascination for Sailor Mars goes beyond mere admiration. *wink*

Jokes aside, it has been a rough Tuesday, and as you navigate through what is to come, I wanted to share this with you. Please know that what she and others feel and think goes beyond you. It extends to generations of cultural erasure; to the burning of our ancestral knowings of queerness being embraced and embroidered into the tapestry of our traditions, beliefs, and stories. Their anger, embarrassment, and insults veiled as humor were never about you. It is their own wounds they get to unravel and sit with, and you cannot fix what is theirs to heal.

But here is the one thing, if nothing else, that I'd want you to hold close, especially on nights when the day's armor can no longer keep the demons at bay:

You will not bring shame to the family.
You are not abnormal for loving a man or a woman.
You do not need to prove your worth.
You are enough.

You will find community, and you will be surrounded by those who hear, see, and deeply love you. They will be your shelter when your own is falling apart.

Know that the battle-hardened saying is true- *things will get better*. And I'll be with you, every jagged step of the way.

With much warmth and unconditional love,
Your Future Self

Magpahinga, Dre - Andre Zarate

Dear Little Andre,

I see you and I am holding you.

You want to belong.
  You want to fit in.
    You want to be loved and appreciated.

But in that little head of yours, you are hearing the multiple voices repeating like a tape recorder. Like in those horror movies when the voices won't get away from you. They are chasing you.

Andre, why are your hands like that?
  Andre, why do you walk like that?
    Andre, why is your voice like that?

Often paired with the same advice –

Man up.
  Clench your first.
    Straighten up your walk.
      Deepen that voice.

The *tsismis*, gossip, of the community repeating the same questions in your head and to their children. Your friends. You are hearing it yourself. You understand Tagalog. Your friends are telling you their parents are asking about you.

So you try to erase that shame. The feeling of not being enough. So you dig and you push. You force yourself to work hard in the one place you can control: School.

Memorizing, memorizing, memorizing.
  Reading, reading, reading.
    Writing, writing, writing.

Trying to be on top.
  Trying to be recognized.
    Trying to be validated.

Because you knew they would say *at least matalino siya,* he's smart.
    And to you, that was enough.
        That was love.

Those long hours,
    those sleepless nights,
        those moments you thought it was resilience.
         those moments you thought you were being *matalino,* smart.

Magpahinga, **rest, Dre.** You are enough.

I love the way you dream. I love the way you imagine.
    I love the way you play with the boundaries of reality and imagination.
        You always went for it.

"Let's play Power Rangers," they say.
    They expect you to choose red, blue, black, or green.

But you choose pink and you love it. I see you moving and dancing. Freely.
Smiling. The way you transformed into that role is everything.

But they rough house you and take the opportunity to beat your ass.
    And you take it for the time being.
        But I love how you continue to pick pink *paulit ulit,* again and again.

Then one day, I saw you try to cover it up. You stopped dreaming and you
stopped imagining. You join sports and some that you do not like. You started
to push yourself beyond physically, mentally, and emotionally.

Run, run, run.
    Throw, throw, throw.
        Push, push, push.

Trying to be on top.
    Trying to be recognized.
Trying to be validated.

Pretending to love hockey and soccer.
    Pretending to be in love with baseball.
        Pretending that this was going to make you more of a *lalaki,* man.

Magpahinga, **rest, Dre.** You are enough.

In school and in church, you learn about love and matrimony, something about those sacraments.

We are supposed to be kind to each other.
    We are supposed to love each other.
        We are supposed to care for one another.
            We are supposed to treat one another with respect.

Except for that homosexuality thing. Now *that* is a sin.
    It's a wrongdoing.
        There's no redemption.
            It's a mistake.
                You're a mistake.

Your peers and classmates are coupling up.
        This girl with that boy. That boy with that girl.
They start making those pairings and they pair you with her.
But you don't feel right inside. She's a great friend, she's a great supporter.

But *he* gives you butterflies –
when he smiles,
    when he talks,
when he reaches out,
    when he calls your name.
        Could he be a crush?

No. Call him bro. Call him friend. Call him foe.
But not your crush,
    but he is.

Keep it silent,
    Keep it low,
        Keep it like he'll never know.

Are you okay?
    Are you sick?
    Are you ill?

Hide, hide, hide.
    Suppress, suppress, suppress,
        Pray, pray, pray
            It all away.

I guess you are right. I do like her.
Trying to be on top.
    Trying to be recognized.
        Trying to be validated.

Magpahinga, **rest, Dre.** You are enough.

The *way* you are always one step ahead of the game.
    Attempting to protect yourself against all of the big scary things:
        Rejection.
            Failure.
                The *feeling* of unworthiness.

All of the accolades give you this sense of value.
    All of the attention gives you this sense of importance.
You long for the tolerance of you.
    You believe tolerance is love.

So you continue to
    Push, push, push.
        Run, run, run.
        Work, work, work.

Trying to be on top.
    Trying to be recognized.
        Trying to be validated.

Andre, as you get older you meet some amazing friends and amazing people,
    who teach you that there is more than tolerance.
        who teach you to show up as all of you.
        who teach you to give yourself permission.

You learn that you get to be who you want to be,
    Love who you want to love,
        And begin to use that imagination again.

So you start to
    Heal, heal, heal.
        Pause, pause, pause.
        Dream. dream. dream.

Trying to stay in the now,
    Trying to just exist,

Trying to love yourself fully.

Sabay tayong magpahinga. Let's rest together.

Pwede ka nang magpahinga, Dre. **You can rest now, Dre.**

With Love,
Big Andre

LESSON THREE

Be critical of your relationship to religion.

To be critical of your relationship to religion is not a call to deny any and all parts. If anything, this is a call to be an actively engaged participant if your choice is to partake in any religious practices. Stay curious rather than blindly accept what has been handed to you. Ask questions and reflect. If at that point it feels right, then you will feel more connected to your faith, the world, and the people around you. You will be in control over what you practice and what you don't practice.

My relationships with religion, spirituality, and science have evolved greatly over the years. Interestingly, as I age, I feel like each of those frameworks of belief, while standing so far apart from one another, are still moving towards the same North Star. That being the truth and the history of humanity's existence and purpose. Engaging with organized religion as a Filipino is complicated, especially while also being queer.

According to a report by the Pew Research Center, as of 2023, 90 percent of Filipino Americans feel close to Christianity either by religious practice or through familial ties and culture. 74 percent of Filipino Americans reportedly practice some form of Christianity (Mohamed & Rotolo, 2023). Indeed, a vast majority (57 percent) of Filipino Americans are practicing Catholics. Though this is down from 65 percent in 2012 (Pew Research Center, 2012), it's still worth mentioning that religion is a huge part of the Filipino experience and by proxy, the *queer* Filipino experience.

I grew up in a semi-religious home in Southern California. My family went to Church nearly every Sunday followed by a regular trip to our closest Home-Town Buffet, which was nestled on the top floor of the Moreno Valley Mall. My brother and I participated in Sunday school and confirmation classes in the space where we spent much of our young childhood lives, the Our Lady of Perpetual Help Church in Riverside, California. I had some fond memories of sitting in a giant beautiful white brick building. Just beyond the entrance the floors and walls were illuminated by colorful stained windows. My brother and I enjoyed picking up donuts from the *church ladies* on our way out of mass. As I entered college after high school, I drifted further away from church, but I maintained several friendships with individuals who were still profoundly connected with their local religious communities. I chose to spend some of my time singing and socializing with my friends who attended and/or performed music at Life Teen events. I accepted invitations to spend time with friends' Christian youth groups. I truly have had wonderful experiences with many of the people I encountered in religious spaces.

Year after year, I consider that there's more and more to appreciate about the mysteries of the universe. Having participated in religious spaces, it is easy for me to see why people are so committed to having faith and practicing faith. What organized religion offers is a sense of belonging through community gathering and community practice; a sense of purpose through ritualistic worship and evangelism; and a sense of peace through knowing what to expect after death whether that belief includes some version of an afterlife or otherwise.

To be clear, I also have some negative memories and feelings towards religious spaces and religious figureheads in my community growing up. My father (who happens to be my number one fan and who these days is openly proud of fathering a queer child) used to berate my brother and I as children if we were unable to recite the Hail Mary or Lord's Prayer by heart. I used to live near one of my childhood friends, a fellow queer Filipino American. Crucifixes adorned their walls. In 2008 my friend's father, who was an ardently Christian man, erected multiple lawn signs advertising, "Yes on 8."

If you were a California resident during this time, you might recognize this lawn sign about the state's Proposition 8 (*Prop 8*), which was on the ballot to add language to the constitution that would ensure marriage would be recognized only between a man and a woman. Aesthetically, it was a delightful little lawn sign. It was bright yellow and included four blue stick figures representing a traditional nuclear family. (Side note: Isn't it interesting how even stick figures are assigned a gender? The stick figures in the dress silhouettes were meant to represent the mother and daughter, and the boxy stick figures were meant to be the father and son.) Prop 8 was a topic of discussion in many settings where religious figures and community members were present. It didn't feel good that this felt at times like an opportunity to dehumanize queer community members; behind the guise of protecting the stick figure children.

I would like to eventually share another (funny-in-hindsight) story with you related to how religion played out in my home, but I will save that for *Lesson Six: Break a Few Rules and Have Fun*. What I want to express at the moment is that conflicting paradigms exist within religious spaces. The interesting dilemma is that what makes organized religion a successful community-building, tight-knit opportunity, is in some ways exactly what makes it problematic for queer Filipinos. Like any other tight-knit community, members are measured by how closely they adhere to group norms and expectations. When norms and expectations include rhetoric or attitudes that do not affirm gender diversity or same-sex marriage, those of us who are queer grapple with internal conflict and self-hatred. I have found in my past experience that organized religion exacerbates some of society's biggest fears; homophobia and transphobia. Consider also that the institution of religion acts as a means to share versions of human history and divine law. If the expectation is that *the word* from these institutions is humanity's law, then it might be used as a tool to police, judge, or shame others into obedience and control.

While the recurring mentions of religion in the letters submitted to With Love have centered on Catholicism and Christianity, it is important to recognize that Filipinos across the diaspora engage in different religious practices. The letters selected for this section of With Love reflect upon and discuss in greater detail, how religion as well as spirituality have impacted their lives as Filipinos in America. Some of these writers encouraged their younger selves to take pause and question religious texts and prayers. Some letters share stories of what it felt like to be the child of prominent leaders in their religious communities. Others wrote about how religious norms may have contributed to their feelings of despair or defeat. Ultimately, these letters do not call for a complete erasure of religion, but recognize the different ways in which we can call upon higher powers for support and how we can continue positively engaging with religious institutions, but with a bit of healthy criticism.

Letter to a Deacon's Kid - Timothy A.M. Tumbokon

Dear Childhood Me,

I have seen, cried, felt pain, and agonized about becoming truly you. I remember the moments living in our white town where you were tokenized for being Filipino, then bullied next for loving men. I have also felt the scars from being different from all my church friends. We went to church camp, thinking you could change for the better. Writing in your journal, crying and wailing to God for being conflicted for loving to watch men fuck and feeling guilty for loving it. The other pain is acknowledging that being gay is not a life for you. The life you want feels like a view from a bridge.

I remember those days when you cried out to God not to change you but to curse him because he cursed you for making you gay and brownish. Every moment of your high school life was a moment of sorrow. Every moment in your middle school life was a painful reminder that you'd never have happiness. In elementary school, you will get tokenized for being Filipino and ostracized for being gay.

Growing up as a deacon's kid did not help; you knew, even though it was not verbalized, that you would live up to expectations. You went to all those youth camps, events on purity culture, and other events. I remember you led some of them. In a sense, to get parental approval. You have never fully earned it. However, your spidey sense tingles, your anxiety telling you that the home you grew up in is not your home. There is another place for you to find the family that will love you and support you.

I know that you always wanted to make your immigrant parents proud of the achievements that you made. Moreso, prove to them that you are worth the pain they went through immigrating here. Every failing grade hurt you; every disappointment made you feel at ease. Measuring up to them and their expectations was not a fun course. Above all the disappointments being you, a homosexual, was one of the highest. I remember the nights when our mom left us in the house alone at age 8 because you were an embarrassment. I also remember when your dad kept correcting you; what you were doing was too femme. The feeling of never enough will be in our hearts; the feeling of being an imposter will stick to you as if it were your scarlet letter. Marking you that any success will not be enough because deep down, you know that they can't love you fully because of the future you wanted.

I, my dear Timothy, I'm living tribute to the fact it will get better each day. At the time I wrote this letter, I was on the cusp of a re-birth. Like when we were baptized in the church bathtub, delivered in the holy water to be renewed in the spiritual being. A higher conscience. That feeling I have for myself. A higher spiritual being. Seeing yourself in the morning and knowing you can love yourself. You can thank Beyonce's *Renaissance* for the added assistance.

The roadless journey is not for everyone. Years and a string of therapy help get you here. Along with your favorite hero Spider-Man, I will tell you that story at a different time. Your therapist helped you deconstruct the moments that hurt you the most. From the words that pierced you like a nail when your mother made backhanded comments about you not being manly enough. To the bullies who made kissing noises behind your back and called you fag on the bus.

Yet, in the end, your pain is your drive to heal the world and will attract. As your therapist of today will tell you, "Your vibe and radiance will attract the people you want around you." It did when you were forced and coerced to come out to your mom. Ultimately, your parents called you trash and worthless to their pains of immigrating here. Your friend group will be your found family. They will love you, and you will love them.

The therapist who you poured your trauma into will tell you *whatever you have is more than enough*. Moreover, Filipino Americans have countless histories of queerness that are revered and considered holy, which is why your tender and loving soul is sacred. The love you have is just so celestial. It is the power to not only love oneself but to love all. I know that we are going to heal the world. There are moments when you feel that won't happen, but remember, I love you. Devotedly. Tenderly.

Before I leave, you will meet your new family, who will love you more than you can imagine. Somedays, you'll call it *the House of Mahal*, the house that love built.

Love,
Timothy A.M. Tumbokon,
The grownup-ish version

P.S: This letter is just a summary of your life and the feelings that I have felt growing up. I will soon write to you more about my life journey.

You Deserve More - Dr. Arnel Calvario Ripkens

Dear 31-Year-Old Arnel Calvario,

Growing up with the homophobic rhetoric and HIV/AIDS stigma of the 80's and 90's made you afraid of being queer growing up. You were completely closed off to the idea.

To be "bakla" was to be ridiculed amongst relatives and you never wanted that kind of attention, so you have done everything you can to avoid this.

You have loved the beautiful music, family tradition, and sense of community growing up as a part of St. Margaret Mary Catholic church, but you are also very cognizant that gay marriage is not supported in Catholicism.

At this point, you already know there is a part of your identity that is queer, and that is wanting to be liberated from this muted version of living.

You have experienced your first gay kiss and it was liberating, but
You are scared,
You are hesitant,
You are overwhelmed,

Please take that leap.

Although it feels like too much and you are afraid of change, you will not be alone in your journey forward.

You have lived your life for others and the expectations you feel they have of you, but YOU DESERVE MORE.

All your loved ones want is for you to live your truth and to be happy.

We are all a brilliant mosaic of many extraordinary parts.

It's time to love the beautiful part of you that is gay.
It's time for you to finally be free.

With Love,
50 Year-Old Dr. Arnel Calvario Ripkens

23 AND ME - BUNNY ANNE

Dear past self,

To be honest, I don't remember much about my past. I'm not going to sit here and lie to you because you need the truth. So I'll come out by admitting that I really only remember the important or most pleasant parts, which I'll clarify, can be independent of one another. Hopefully, you'll realize that *joy* is vitally important too. As embarrassed as I am to showcase my wisdom, I'll inform you that while we are not all we'd like to amount to now, we were only further away from self-actualization before.

Joy, not necessarily "happiness," for the word "happiness" often is preceded by some form of "chase." Joy in the present discomforts. In the present half-full glass of water when you, in eternity, are perpetually thirsty. Acknowledgement of how much you need to fill, but enjoyment of the part you have right now.

I'm hearing a more valiant, tenable voice in my head echoing, "For the sake of the story."

Limerence. Does that ring a bell for you, or are you still stuck in your head in musical limbo? I can almost hear your response now. *I hope she's only mean to me.* You're always so nice to others even though you don't feel responsible for being nice to yourself.

I'd like to think so too, young Bunny. And I can't blame you. Because you are not going to help yourself anytime soon with, you know, your very essential hierarchy of needs that you keep insisting is the least of your problems but is, in fact, and I'm shyly and internally shaking my head at the obviousness of this, the most important of your problems. How are we going to function every single day without prioritizing our rest?

Polyamory and *pansexuality.* Remember wanting to have fun with everyone, not just one person? You're polyamorous. And that's okay despite the taboo because you'll be honest with your future partners about it, and it'll be consensual. You're also pansexual, because you don't want to do stuff with just boys, and believing in the binary intrinsically hurts you in that you have to enforce a narrative of this-or-that, a worried voice in your head constantly debating: *Is this too masculine or too feminine?* And so naturally, after learning more about intersex people, and that 1.7 percent of the world is intersex (at least judging by our late prerequisites in gender categorization), you have a suspicion you might've been born intersex. All those comments from family members that your coochie is too big? Bam. You're intersex. Perfect explanation. Now, I'm not sure that I am intersex, but 1.7 percent of the world is; and that's more than 100 million people. That's a lot.

Also, to the Bunny who started writing this a couple of days ago: Why do you think you must be sad or miserable to write sufficiently? Who are you mostly serving here? Yourself. So if you're having fun writing this, don't stop yourself. Don't make yourself cry. God, I love beating myself up, so don't do it for me! Speaking of God...Let me tell you a story about you/me.

"What's that?" 12-year-old me asked. A sunbleached resin statuette stood approximately two feet tall on the shelf of the open west-facing window, dozens of beaded baptism party favors scattered about her feet under her yellowing white robe. Afternoon light poured in, penetrating the squinting Venetian blinds and illuminating the dust nestled in her crevices.

"Our Virgin Mary!" my mother exclaimed.

"Who?"

"I can't believe you don't know Virgin Mary. You don't listen during church?"

I shrugged.

"Don't mistake her for Mary Magdalene, because she is bad. Okay, anak?"

I gave an unsure nod as I trod downstairs to grab our chihuahua Jacob — I mean, Kush — to bring him to the store with us. *Mary Magdalene sounds cool*, I thought to myself.

So, this is my symbolic scenario. Like I said, I'll be transparent with you. Which parts of it are actual events that took place? 97%. I'll break up the lies. 1% is what your mother told you about Catholicism, since I can't recall much of what she taught me about religion if she talked to me about it at all. But if she did say something, I would bet $20 (hey, the going's tough despite your efforts to speedily sail through college and work as hard as you can to be financially independent as soon as possible) that it was about Virgin Mary being the good one and the cool statue and Mary Magdalene being bad and having no statue. Another 1% makes up for the fact that we didn't even really go to church except on Easter and Christmas, and were still about half an hour late each time. But I'm not mad about that. The final 1% is the fact that mini baby blue or pink rosaries were scattered at the altar. They weren't, but there were stacks of rosaries draped around the Virgin Mary's neck. Displaying party favors was what the curio cabinet in the dining room was for. Mind you, this was 2011, when you were 11 and just underwent a D.A.R.E. presentation and pledge at school, so we hadn't learned the healthy benefits of the then-heavily stigmatized Mary Jane yet. So I was keen on calling the dog my older brother and his girlfriend adopted, "Jacob." Post-high, I refer to him as Kush Jacobs. Lola and I loved the dog.

Still, these are the fond memories we haven't pushed out of our head, and although I love the genre, I would love to spare you the coming-of-age times we had with her more recently during our teen years that our brains desperately scramble to forget. But those still lie embedded in my mind like a fresh cut, or more literally, a bruise.

And there we go. Now that I have you, I guess I will indulge to divulge. (By all means, scan through the next couple of paragraphs since you're pretty much familiar with the whole traumatized child shtick already. Actually, why not the whole bit? It's not much to us anymore anyway. But the mere act of me even writing about this is for...frankly, it's more for me. It's for the both of us, assuming I'm still writing to you, my younger self.)

We love Lola. She bathed and fed you as a little girl, and kept cooking and cleaning at home so that Mom could go to work. We look up to her for teaching us love through domestic devotion. She communicated this love by sacrificing all of her waking hours for us, from dawn to midnight every day, bustling around the house from one task to the next. She mastered all of this so well that she was able to do this throughout her seventies and eighties, never really complaining, although it would only occasionally slip out that her knees hurt. Lola was a homemaker at heart. She taught us that the art of work-life balance had to bleed into one another at some point, so that one didn't become deranged with... an unstable sense of identity.

However in and out of reality she was, Mom was brisk and careful like a ticking borderline time bomb pattering from her 9 to 5 to the casino and quickly back to work with a brisk shower, a dab of makeup, three pumps each of various per-fumes, and a few shrieking, swinging hours of early morning child vilification to prime herself. I'm proud of her for being there for me half as much as Lola was. The fact that my mom diligently got herself up by 6 in the morning, took as much overtime as she could get, bought me clothes, and took me to Barnes & Noble was reasonable enough to have me whipped into the tyrannical grip of the love bomb. I would rather not go into great detail about her abuse of power to spare you the suffering, since I believe you are in enough pain already. If you think I'm mean about Mom, remember her ruthfulness towards her own mother. You aren't 100% crazy. Albeit, no one knows for sure what reality is, but since no one knows, you have the power to validate yourself. Your experiences are real. Lola knows this. You both shared the damage of someone who hurt themselves so much that they had to hurt others. And while you can't learn everything at once and effectively use what you know, at least you learn.

Dad was kind enough to give me his last name. I do feel bad for my mom because I don't think he helped out with money at all, with his hav-ing-a-wife-and-three-daughters-in-another-house-and-all, but hey! At least he checked in twice a year at 11 pm on a weekday with a group of friends and some shiny foil. She barely convinced him to see me that these semi-annual get-to-gethers counted as a great success. Better yet, after your fatherless childhood and your mom's partnerless child-rearing, when you turned 15, Mom managed to rent a room when Dad got the *bota* out of his wife's house. He was so good at this that it happened to him again and again between city rehab and our room. Nights on what you might otherwise consider a sizable queen-sized bed with the king, queen, and princess tucked under the royal blanket, with the highness himself conked out next to empty pen barrels. Good for him. He must've done a lot of writing.

Spoiler alert: We are still mad at our parents. If this sounds anything like you, just take comfort in the fact that we can indeed leave them one day despite the common Filipino value of putting family first, *no matter what*. Nothing is absolute. While upholding the value of pacifism, to effectively exist it must feel aggressive to be yourself.

You are doing amazing for being honest with yourself about your feelings. You're still amazing. And you don't beat yourself up because you deserve it, but because it's fun to beat someone up sometimes and you're not hurting anyone but yourself. And obviously, because your mom conditioned you (either as an intended or latent function of sewing you into her fabric of reality) constant doubt and worry are how things are supposed to feel. Your feelings are reason-able and valid. Just remember the voice telling you it's worth it for the sake of the story. The truths are aplenty and simultaneously true, but taking one step at a time is the most you can do.

Just because one's behavior or actions are understandable doesn't mean they're justifiable. Hey, you have a knack for sensing the answers and understanding the reasons, but you're always so doubtful of yourself. The answer is in the stone, okay? You, underneath it all, know what it looks like. It's just always hard to carve it.

It's okay to be curious about feminism. I know you're embarrassed of your phases no matter if you consider any reason why so-called "liberal" topics are bad. Who defines "liberal" after all? Who defines "bad" after all? Today's conservatism is yesterday's liberal. And yes, little rebel you are correct about "bad" being something made up to keep society orderly and functioning. It made sense that you grew cautious of your actions after years of your mother nitpicking your flaws, and stayed skeptical of your coping mechanism to identify with feminism, and after getting into your first serious relationship with a Christian Korean-American boy who wouldn't accept you unless you became Christian and promised not to tan your skin any darker, and whose own mother did not want to accept you either. What's the deal with moms having a problem with you? You are so not going to become Cinderella's evil mother. And I say "mother," not "stepmother," because in the original fairytale, it's her biological mother. And just because you had issues with your mom which left a mother-shaped hole in your heart, it doesn't mean you aren't a feminist.

Hint: You're still entranced by Catholicism and Christianity because Christian religions are so prevalent in our past and living history. You will find inspiration behind Jesus through a more Gnostic approach to Christianity, but this doesn't mean that all the answers lie there because existence is beyond organized religion. The word "religion" comes from the Latin *religare*, which means "to bind." No need to be stubbornly attached to any one thing in particular. Which is why we're polyamorous! Don't forget to acknowledge your responsibility for yourself, and as much as you love to drag yourself, autoamory is a part of all of this too. Autoamory, in my words, is one's love for themself. Not just the token self-care bath or some yoga, but the energy behind one's actions. The personal intention of why one does the things they do.

Yes, we are still afraid of putting ourselves out there as a queer creature of color. I'm better at loving myself, but you are the best at trying things for the first time. You are beautiful in your youth not because you have the least wrinkles and the largest thigh gap we'll ever have (I slightly envy you but would a hundred times over choose my peace of gut over the stress and delusional thinking of skinny culture), but because you are unafraid to handle your first pains of everything. Your courage to be ostracized is marvelous. Take this moment while you can, and I'll take my moments while I can.

Of course, there are ups and downs, but you have the responsibility to make your own ups because circumstance and chaos theory will make the downs for you. Manifest, or take into your own hands as much as you can, but also *wu wei* your energy and be at peace with how you won't feel like doing something productive every day and just let the pieces that are relentlessly falling fall gracefully.

Maybe you are still learning to love yourself. I shouldn't call you out because I'm still learning to love myself as I'm writing this. I am not so far removed from my childhood trauma yet myself, and trying to tie my personal story into a digestible narrative with a relatable character is a first, but hopefully not the last chance for us. We are still in the process of learning to love ourselves through appreciating others born and raised like us, and realizing, despite our differences in gender expression and sexuality, that there are too many differences to count. What counts is our alikeness. We are brought together by the comfort of common racial ancestry, culture, and geography, but we leave this story knowing we are part of the world. However we may be taught to conform to fully belong, especially as Filipinos, we are already, by corollary, belonging.

Love,
Bunny

P.S. Dear future Bunny, you're going to read this letter and see exactly how you could've written this more concisely. I just hope that instead of beating yourself up every day, you're able to put that energy towards actually exercising to improve most days. Because wasting your time beating yourself up gives you more reason to beat yourself up. Break this generational cycle.

10-YEAR RECAP - MJ BH

Dear Younger MJ,

It's been 10 years. I wish I could say that things have gotten better; because that's what we're told, right? "It gets better." But for who, exactly? Let's take a stroll down *Memory Lane*... 10 years ago, you "came out" to your family, emphasis on the air quotes. It has become one of the most vivid memories that I can recall in an instant. Sitting at the kitchen counter, the center of it all, almost as if you were being interrogated for something you did wrong. But what exactly did you do wrong? Drugs? Alcohol? Get into a fight with someone? No. Your parents discovered how to access social media. Yet the one post that had nothing to do with your sexuality brought more and more questions, to the point of the winning question of the night: *Are you gay?*

Now, what you actually told them is a bit of a blur, because we tend to block out traumatic experiences. I recall the mention of "his" name (Your first boy crush. Ugh). Trying to explain what I was experiencing and bring light to my perspective on the next winning question *"Why are you gay?"* was definitely a memory for the books. I found it easier to defend my doctoral dissertation than having to explain to my very conservative family "why I was gay," as if I had a choice in the matter.

Why do you love the K-Pop group, Seventeen? Because I love how their music makes you feel, their dancing is impeccable, and they are an attractive group (I wish you discovered them sooner, but better later than never). *Why do you love to cook?* Discovering new dishes, cultures, and it brings people together. Food is life, duh. *Why do you love playing the piano?* Despite being forced to take lessons as a kid, I grew to love the instrument; it has become my safe space for emotional expression and meditation, and it has brought me opportunities to meet people of the same passion and build a community around it. *So why are you gay?* I ... just am.

You think the conversation ended right then and there? Think again, because that conversation lasted for another 3-4 hours. But it wasn't just about trying to understand what I was going through (that barely lasted). Somehow the conversation became about *them*. "What did I do wrong? When and where did I go wrong? What did I do to deserve this?" Of course, someone always has to mention that it was because I went to *that* school. Because going to a specific school turns you gay, right?

For parents who were so focused on Americanizing our family, you can't help but think that they tend to fall back into what we consider the "typical Filipino parents." It wasn't finding a spouse to love for the rest of your life, but someone young enough who will take care of you when you get older. It wasn't about having kids of your own and experiencing the joys of parenthood, but giving your parents some grandchildren they can brag about to their friends and relatives. Career building? No, it's the question of how much money you will be making to be able to support yourself. And here's the kicker – *No one will hire you if they know you're gay* (their words, not mine).

Here's a somewhat positive outcome - You'll find that our parents do have some basic understanding of mental health, which is not as common in the typical Filipino household. But you have to remember that you grew up in a Christian home with a PK (Pastor's Kid) who now does not believe in any of it. So now you know why life has been a challenge. How do you follow a belief system that was taught to you, yet you have a parent who goes against it? What DO you believe? But rather, maybe the question is … what do YOU believe?

If there is one takeaway to summarize these past 10 years, it's learning that you are your own person. You have your friends and family to lean on for support (whether they know you're gay or not), but at the end of the day, you decide what happens with your life. You are in control of who you choose to let in about your true self. You are in control of where you want your career to go, and your sexuality does not dictate where you find yourself. (This is contrary to what you were told. Yes, working at a faith-based organization has its challenges.) As much as you have your faith, you can't wait for things to happen, and He knows that.

If only I had realized all this sooner, maybe things would've been different. I wish I could give you a big hug to hopefully make things better. But that's another thing - it's not about what happened in the past, but what actions you take to move forward with life. It may not have to be a big step, and sometimes growth and progress mean just being present. Challenges will come, and they continue to happen one way or another. But progress is still progress, and you'll get to where you want to be in time, whether it's in personal growth, love life, or maybe even with your family. I love you, and buckle up – you're in for one hell of a ride.

Take care,
Dr. MJ

Temporary Darkness - Lani Fontillas

Dear Little Lani,

You may not have an answer when people ask how you identify. Your peers will call you "the Asian Tomboy girl who plays sports." At home, your mom will question why you dress like a boy or why your hair is never down, but the "other" clothes never really fit. Your mom will find you an Asian basketball league in an attempt to find a place of likeness in your predominantly Caucasian town. And yet as a Filipino, you still don't quite fit in because you aren't Asian enough. You'll question yourself as to why the boys don't like you like other girls, and you'll agree to like them back if they like you. As you get older, you'll find relationships that warm your insides, and it's usually with another girl from the sports teams. You'll think you want to be like these girls, but I'll tell you what that feeling is. It's fondness. When you're 17, you'll get a friend you feel like you can't live without. She will be your first love. Like you, she'll never have felt this way about anyone else either. With the anger and fear of being "gay," you'll hide all of these feelings from the outside world, and you'll question what living is worth.

Coming from a Catholic Filipino family, you'll hold your secret inside, and you'll even resent yourself for having such feelings, but this won't be forever. One day you'll be forced to come out, and your dad will say things that will cut your insides out, but know these are just words. One day your traditional Catholic Filipino family will understand what's truly important. They will slowly embrace you, and your relationships and learn to love your partner. Although you will grow up in the dark about what it means to be gay and what it feels like to be accepted for who you are, the lights will turn on and you will learn to live life as your authentic self. One day you'll get on one knee and ask the woman of your dreams to marry you, and you'll start planning a wedding and making a family with her. Your parents will support your union, offer to help pay for it, and even joke about when they will have grandkids. Little Lani, being in the dark can be hard, but do what you have to do to survive. When you're ready, take on the world with strength and remain true to yourself. Your family and friends may take a while to understand who you are, but in the end, they will be by your side!

With Love,
Lani, A Happily Engaged Woman (Married May 18, 2024)

Stop Those Hail Marys for a Second and Listen - P. M.

Hey,

Stop those Hail Marys for a second and listen. You will not die of AIDS for crushing on the football captain. You won't disgrace your family because you love and desire who you love. You're going to be fabulous. It's still hard to believe it. I've been celebrating every moment when I feel grateful for being alive: The partner that supported you for the past 19 years. The younger sister you helped raise is a beautiful soul working through her own traumas. The traumas that you tried to lighten up when you wrote that letter to Dad after high school graduation. You wrote, "I don't respect you." You added, make it better for her.

You will be loved and desired. You will learn to take care of yourself. You will learn to pray for strength instead of erasure. You will find many more higher energies to ask for guidance. The stars, the ancestors, they watch over you.

P.M.

JESS LIKE YOU - JESSICA LUSTINA AFABLE

Dear Jessica,

At 6 years old, some may think it's weird that you always love to wear your first pair of Jordans. How could they understand that you get to wear basketball greatness in the form of sleek 13s? Your sneakers may not complement the dresses lined with frills and stockings that mom dresses you in. And you can't seem to avoid the jokes of the other Filipino kids at church who call you names like "tomboy." But who's Tom? And I'm not a boy. You are your father's adventurous daughter, Jessica naneng (*"naneng" an Ilocano/Tagalog term of endearment for a younger female*). The one who loves to play outside, whistle, constantly catches creepy critters beyond the backyard screen door, and chooses that blue Hercules lunchbox over all the pink ones with Daisy Duck.

Your childhood years will go by like the photo strips of annual school pictures that will be so evident of you looking like a cute Filipina Alex Mack. Dad will help you slick your hair back with gel, just like Manong (*manong meaning "older brother" in Ilocano and Tagalog*) does it, but in a ponytail. You'll compromise with Mom and wear the dangly earrings she loves and a Pocahontas T-shirt because we love Pocahontas. But this won't stop Mom from constantly telling you that whistling is only for boys, and she's not a fan of your clothes and how you cut your hair. Maybe this was her way of assimilating to the "American culture," so you played the part and tried "girly" things with your cousins, like having "matching-matching" clothes, hair, makeup, and a love for boy bands. You are a beautifully happy kid, even if you feel awkward in your clothes and body. You will discover dance one day. And dance will help you feel more comfortable as you learn to live and move in your body and being.

By 16, there will be another Filipina girl on your basketball team, and the only thing she'll remember you by is that beloved family nickname–Jeca. But you'll never forget that you two were in a Christian club together or that she was an amazing basketball player...or that she had a beautiful smile and perfect hair. And, I think you like her...like her. Admitting this to yourself and others may come off as, "Yeah, I think she's really cool." When you think she's *so* pretty, you'll do almost anything to be her friend. This is where unrequited crushes begin. So, to your tender heart, good luck. You'll also spend hours waiting for a girl online to feel "closer" to her. But, in person, you're just the girl who drives her home one night. You'll wish you could tell her she ruined dimpled smiles for you.

As you come of age, you'll date a good amount of guys, and the hard part isn't the breakups. It'll be everything leading up to them. It's changing, then losing yourself to be "the perfect girl" they want. In the back of your mind, you'll count how long you can keep a good guy in your life. But when feelings intensify, you ghost them, like your true feelings, and say, "I'm sure you'll be better off without me." You'll ultimately feel broken and guilty for deceiving them and yourself for being a *pretty* shell of a person. Not only does this play out terribly for your self-worth as a girl who feels like she's only meant for the male fantasy, but as an overall growing human. Then, one day, you'll learn to thank the last guy you dated. He was the first one to question your queerness. He was right about you being head over heels for the girl he thought you liked. You'll face this meaningful conversation alone in your college dorm room one day or when you realize that not everyone thinks the Victoria's Secret Fashion Show is equivalent to the Super Bowl like you do.

In your 20s, you'll constantly struggle with how to live life as a queer Christian, and being within those two communities that don't always see things *queerly*. You'll tend to feel like a "closeted queer" and a "closeted Christian," never truly enough for either community. Because of this, you'll feel lonely and find it hard to be resilient. For a girl who prays with open hands, you'll often catch yourself walking through the world with fists up or hands up in surrender on days when fear feels synonymous with gravity and you agree with the saying, "I'm scared to death." You believe in the power of words—even the hurtful ones. But bravery will redirect your understanding of where and how you need to grow. You'll be told that self-care isn't just about pampering one's self. It also includes difficult moments, like stepping away from people and places that hinder and hurt you. And as you search tirelessly for love and belonging in people and places you wish reflected the rainbows in your life, you'll eventually find those who live bravely and hold the same identities.

Although you may feel broken at times, you'll still be the one who lives with unconditional compassion, love, and understanding for the world we wish would embrace us in the same way. You'll also be met with allies and safe spaces you will hold dear. They'll help you lower your armor and meet you with vulnerability. On days that feel impossible, you will remember each person who truly knows you. With a whole heart and eyes welled with tears of joy, their words and comfort will carry you. You will have a world that will see the real you. It'll feel reflective, validating, and loving.

A life full of rainbows and smiles is tangible, even God made covenants with them. *Gayborhoods* will feel like Disneyland. Friends will become family. You'll find and adore music, books, clothes, and content that represent you. You'll eventually stop hiding all these things that make you genuinely happy and begin to share them. And someday, you'll buy pretty girls flowers and tell them they're gorgeous. You'll allow yourself to lean in, hold their gaze, and hold their hand down the street. Even now, I hope you allow yourself to get giddy and not shy away from your blushing smiles. You'll feel peace one day. The endless nights, drives, and sleepless train rides will cease. You'll find love and a best friend in a beautiful girl who sees all of you, who holds your heart, brings you rest, and becomes your home. And this is when you finally learn what it's like to be in love.

Every day, you'll wish you knew someone "Jess" like you; one to look up to. But healing will look like being that person you've longed for. She will lead the way for a girl who can now dress and address herself. One who stands on both feet, suited in greatness.

Sincerely,
The girl in her Jordans

LESSON FOUR

Your parents were doing what they knew. Take it or leave it.

My older brother's name is Michael; we were born only about 18 months apart. When he became a father, we were in our early 30s. Michael shared the news with me by phone that he had a little one on the way. He didn't tell me he was excited, but I could hear it in his voice. This was one of the happiest moments of his life. I recall joking with him that it felt crazy that he was going to be responsible for another human life when it was painfully obvious that we were still figuring out how to manage our own lives.

To give us a bit of credit, we were both living independently; we were both working full-time; and we were both paying our bills. We were certainly responsible adults; we still are. There's just something different about being entirely responsible for the outcomes and upbringing of another human being. It's an immense responsibility. As I've noted already in Lesson Two, beware of perfectionism. If it's unfair to expect this of ourselves, should we expect perfection from others, let alone our parents?

Even after I finished college and early into my professional career, I didn't feel *grown up*. Perhaps part of this feeling came from the fact that I was always encountering some new challenge or problem to which I didn't already have a solution. Should I have *everything* figured out to be considered a grown-up? No. I guess that's the secret to adulthood, there's always something we've got left to figure out.

· ♥ · ♥ · ♥ · ♥ · ♥ ·

For queer Filipinos in America, our relationships with our parents are complicated at best. Expectations we have of our parents and the expectations our parents have of us are influenced by several social factors that exist in the United States and the Philippines. Expectations of gender, sexuality, and religion are some of the most prominent factors.

Perhaps for many families in the Philippines, one might observe more egalitarian leaning norms in comparison to families with long histories in the United States. Regardless, expectations based on gender still exist. For example, Filipino mothers often take on most of the responsibilities of child-rearing; while Filipino fathers will intervene generally when a child has committed a serious infraction (Blair, 2014). Filipino mothers may resort to minimal means of physical punishment; Filipino fathers are seen as the primary disciplinarian and they are more likely to use physical forms of punishment. We can expect that socialization of these gender norms will manifest itself in how parents will raise their daughters versus their sons. In the letters throughout this book, and especially those presented in this chapter, you may notice how some of our writers experienced conflict due to the policing of gender and sexuality by either parental figures or other adults close to the family.

Catholicism, being one of the heavy-hitting organized religions for Filipinos in the Philippines and Filipinos in the United States, impacts how large our families even become. Catholicism is a pro-natalist religion (Blair, 2014). In effect, Filipino Catholics (and Filipinos of other similar religious denominations) are culturally expected to not only get married but also have tons of babies. It's an overdone trope on social media at this point to see a video of younger Filipinos pretending to be their *tita* or *nanay* exclaiming, "Do you have a boyfriend now? Are you going to have babies? When? *Anak*, soon!"

Reasonably because of traditional mindsets and misinformation, when/if we come out to our Filipino parents as queer, it's likely that one of the immediate resulting concerns is that we cannot get married nor can we raise children. I can tell you from having been to multiple queer and same-sex weddings, that marriage is in fact on the table for us in modern society if we so choose it. I have also encountered plenty of queer individuals who have birthed and/or raised both biological children and adopted children. There are many ways in which family units can begin and continue; stay tuned for *Lesson Five: Find your chosen family.*

For now, let's return to a focus on parent-child relationships. Researchers would say that greater parental involvement, taking more action, and feeling a sense of responsibility towards the experiences that socialize the child are associated with more positive outcomes. For example, parents who volunteer at their children's schools make the family more well-known in the community and may strengthen the child's future social capital.

Multiple studies have shown that the quality of the relationship between parent and child will affect the mental health and educational outcomes of the child, especially for Filipinos and other Asians in the United States (Blair, 2014; Warikoo et al., 2014). But what would *you* say is the measure of a high-quality relationship? How would it differ from what your parent(s) might say? And if you have children, what would your children say? From being parented by my parents and from observing my brother and cousins who have become parents, I've concluded that both children and parents have evolving needs and desires as they age. Think of rules that promote safety. Think of routines that promote a predictable and therefore comfortable everyday life. These are necessary, but at times feel confining for both the child and the parent.

My personal feeling is that a high-quality, parent relationship between parent-child includes respect, trust, and the freedom to explore as well as express. I believe these should be afforded to both parents and children. We are all human and we all make mistakes, yet that's not an excuse to continue adding fuel to the flame of an abusive relationship if that's how you might characterize your relationship with your parents (or children). We all also have the capacity and the responsibility to grow, learn, as well as repair if our goal is to foster healthy and positive relationships.

· ♥ · ♥ · ♥ · ♥ · ♥ ·

Michael is a wonderful brother and I love him dearly. I feel he is one of the few people in this world who truly respects and understands my evolving perspectives when it comes to being a queer Filipino son. Listening to him talk about parenthood and watching him figure out how to parent completely reframed my relationship with our mother and father. He's doing the best he can based on what he and the mother of his children know were effective and kind strategies for them. They make mistakes, but they are trying desperately to do better than previous generations. I can't help but think that every generation of parents has some flaws, but parenting gets just a little bit better every generation based on the lessons learned from being parented.

The letters featured in this section reflect the complex and nuanced emotions and histories the writers have with their parents. In some letters, writers reflect on their parent's attempts to develop relationships and impart wisdom, though perhaps unwarranted or misinformed. In other letters, you find writers recounting their desires to overcome and call out the abuse and ignorance from parental figures. In some letters, writers attempt to reach inner peace after reflecting on well-intended mistakes made by their parents in the past.

LOVING BY THE BOOK - ALYSSA B.V. CAHOY

Langga,

On your 18th birthday, your mother will gift you with a book entitled *Adulting 101: #Wisdom4Life* (2018).

That would be the first and last time you held that book in your hands. Neither you nor your mother will mention that book in the years to come, but I have been thinking about it more frequently these days.

How you sought out life in desperation, after years of deferring American-only angst.

When life invariably diverged from what the book had to say, and practice became Teacher.

What the exchange of that book told you about the mediated
                 love between
Pinay mothers   and   daughters.

You have to learn how to read

closely to be able to

recognize the depth, the

history, of that love.

Now that I look back, I think that was our mother's way of slipping us some #RealTalk about taboo subjects and other life things she had to figure out on her own (i.e., the hard way), like saving money, finding a life partner, and so forth.

The book— a conduit for maternal love and generational knowledge.

Barbara Jane Reyes, a Filipina poet and educator (whose collections you will turn to when you feel hemmed in by life and need to find the language to articulate your experiences), wrote in her book *Wanna Peek Into My Notebook?:*

Notes on Pinay Liminality (2022) about the personal and collective politics of reckoning with a Pinay identity, with particular regard to mother-daughter relationships:

> As Pinays, we constantly resist silence; many of us know the pain of having been mothered by silenced women. From within a culture of we, silence can be construed as consent, and dissent as an inconvenience, an undesirable alien element undermining consensus and community. (57-8)

The colonial mentality forcefully bred into our culture will dictate which things are better left unsaid, and yet, they can be written and passed down. Writing is *resistance* to silence. *Reading* is resistance to silence. Your mother gave you a means to resist silence on your 18th birthday.

You will encounter the most disquieting silence in your immediate family, and you are the designated Disturber of Peace. (Is it peace, or is it just silence? Are you Disturber of Peace, or are you just awaiting a PTSD diagnosis?) Nevertheless, you will have unmasked yourself and come into your own vibrant personhood: unlocking an unexpected inner goofiness that tempers your pensiveness; queering business-casual apparel with fake food earrings and platform shoes; keeping the critical thinking cap on even when you're inside the house.

There is much transformative healing ahead. Your mother, while open-minded, will feel at a loss for how to reach you.

She will tiptoe   around   you   , not wanting to risk adding to your spinning plates. You may find yourself wanting to interpret her reluctance as silence.

You will learn to distinguish stillness from silence. Your mother speaks quite incisively in other ways. She had to, and she has since been a woman of few words.

Your mother, too, was given a book to live by. Except her book wasn't called *Adulting 101*; it was called *The Holy Catholic Bible*. She attended girls-only schools administered by nuns and studied the sacred book in earnest. Eventually, she sought God beyond the Catholic church.

Even though it has been over two decades since she recited Hail Marys during

Sunday mass, she still knows the verses by memory. She shares them with me in moments of despair.

From her mouth pours the wellspring of her heart.

Deep waters flow quietly.

I had to learn how to read

closely to be able to

recognize the depth, the

history of that love.

In the directory of an old comb-bound booklet for a clan reunion decades ago, your mother was given the epithet "machine gun"— Machine Gun Armi. I chuckled then, thinking it an apt name. Having a sharp conscience even as a teenage girl, she is a nanay with discerning wisdom, her own special tea blend of encouragement, harvested from fields of labor, and dried in the sunlight of aging.

Your mother has paved the path for you thus far, and you are starting to walk in step with her.

You are speaking through the page.

That is how you can reassure your mother you are loving by the book, so to speak, that she gifted you on your 18th birthday.

Yours truly,
Ysa who is to come

BADGE OF HONOR – RESI IBAÑEZ

Dear Isa,

Don't worry about that other name you hate. The one of the statue who stares you down every night from the top of your dresser drawers.

You will have to fight for it, you will have to save up money for it, but you can change it.

You will have to deal with white people butchering it, saying crap like *oh, that sounds exotic.* Sure, you will have a photo album on your phone (yes, phones in the future can take pictures and hold albums) of names like "Grizzy" or "Frizzy" that baristas write on coffee cups when they misunderstand you.

But you delight in the humor of it. Even the worst butchering is better than the name you have right now, the one you feel like you're stuck with. The one you shrug your shoulders about because you're tired of having to try on different names to feel right, but you don't know what else to do.

At some point, you will learn a word for the screeching halting feeling you have whenever you hear the name you hate out loud: Dysphoria. When you feel like you're gnawing on glass every time you say it, when you feel like you're in a burning hailstorm whenever you hear it, do you really have to answer to that name? No, you don't.

Stay curious. Take German in college (yes, you make it to college) to learn about that side of your heritage. Studying German will lead you to the name you have as an adult, the one you will legally change your name to.

And it leads to a surprise. Your nanay, whose name you never knew while she was alive, ends up finding you with your new name too. After you find your name, your mom shows you a photo of your nanay from the late 1940s. It is a black and white portrait, with scalloped edges, taken in a photo studio. She wears a white dress with her initials appliqued or embroidered by her shoulder. She has white pumps on, her shoulder-length black hair in ringlets, with a white flower pinned.

On the back, she wrote a note to your tatay, and signed it "Resing." Your mom points out, *ng* is a suffix. Which means she also was Resi. Her full name, Rizalina.

Named after a freedom fighter.

In high school, you listen to *American Idiot* by Green Day. You save up what you earned from weeks of babysitting and coaching the landlord's kid on their piano lessons, all to afford a $30 studded belt from Hot Topic. You listen to My Chemical Romance sing songs about death, memory, and carrying on. You love punk music, but you don't feel like you're angry enough to be punk.

But when you change your name, it's the most punk thing you'll ever do. You change your middle name too. Your mother gave you a middle name after a tita you never met, one who died, whose name translated to sorrow.

But you change it to the thing that, in the end, takes your mother's life. And paradoxically, it's the same thing that keeps you alive. The same thing people power brought to life in the Philippines. Your heart.

Your middle name means freedom. It means love. It brings down dictators.

Years later, your white father will say your new name means snowflake. He means it as an insult.

Take it as a badge of honor.

You are your own freedom fighter.

Keep loving, keep fighting,
Resi

LEAVE YOUR ABUSER - BUNNY ANNE

Dear past self,

If I could go back in time and tell you: don't wait until you're a legal adult to leave your mom. Don't wait to leave your family. She's going to threaten you against the idea, knowing what she's doing is wrong, to say the least. She'll say all the parents are doing it, like her actions are as harmless as trying hot new trends in art and fashion. If you stay with her, she'll make you distrust your emotions until you doubt your gut's first instincts.

At age 18, you'll go to therapy for the first time. Not because your mother encouraged you to go, but because you finally mustered up the courage to seek help. You'll tell yourself and Mom that it's to overcome your needle phobia, because looking after your physical health seems more normal than looking after your mental health, and because you're in denial of your subconscious telling you that you need an outsider's point of view of the havoc at home.

Your therapist will listen and find out (and not easily, because she'll have to pry the truths of abuse your family conditions you to hide) that the reason you're there is not just because of trypanophobia, but also because of the fear that your own mother will never get better. That she will never treat you better. Violence and emotional abuse, casually continuing to be an everyday routine, day after day...

Your therapist will say, "You could have called the authorities to take you out of that home because what your mother did is a crime."

You'll look surprised.

"But you're 18 now which means you can't get help because you're legally an adult."

A moment will pass as the thought sinks in. Unnerved, you'll look for hope that maybe...maybe people change. Her next line hits you like a bus you regularly wait for but never take. She looks at you with a commiserative expression. The therapist watches your face and softly repeats herself, unsure if you got on board. "I don't think she will ever stop." At which point you'll uncontrollably burst into the tears you pent up over the years, mad at your mother and angry at yourself for not seeking help sooner.

When you're 19, you'll meet a wonderful girl your age who grew up without her biological parents and say, "Being an orphan is the best. The government pays for my living until I'm older." She's a legal adult too, but it's just that she went into the system way younger. She knew what she was doing, and you'll admire her for being brave enough to leave her dangerous situation sooner in life.

The earlier you call for help, the sooner you'll realize you don't owe people who weren't just raising you, but were raising you to owe them your life. There are already too many things holding you back in society with your cultural identifiers because even in 2023, your male Filipino counterparts still struggle in a late-stage capitalist patriarchy that's as predominantly intersectional as the second wave of feminism in the United States. You need to aggressively be yourself. Keep aggressively being yourself, even when the shame of making mistakes hits. Being "perfect" will never happen, but wasting time beating yourself up when others inevitably do it for you can. Change. Adapt.

The people who claim to be your loved ones, your family, maybe even your friends, are going to displace their bitterness onto you in even the most hurtful ways if you let them, because we are animals. We are humans. You must unapologetically take resources as they're given, especially since it's hard to be taken seriously given what you look like. Even in 2023, females will be widely scapegoated as the crazy, dumb animals that must reassume their subservient roles after being negligently given too much power after a resurgence in male sympathy and neotraditionalism — and not the cool tattoo style. The stereotype you are born into the can and will be used against you, by strangers and by people closest to you.

If it's too late and the old software continues to be used in our new system, find little ways to rebel. If you are such a lover, put your love towards someone who will gratefully return it tenfold per their abundance of resources. People who don't care much for your achievements will guilt you by saying they laid the groundwork for you to walk upon. You simply express your gratitude, and move on, because what more are they asking for? Yes, we are all part of one, but you are born an individual to be an individual. You can become one with the universe again when you die.

With love,
Bunny

I Understand - Rana Rosanes

Hey younger Rana,

I know this is weird. You're probably thinking, "Why is my future self taking the time out of her day to write to her younger self?" First of all, I agree. It is weird! Secondly, everything is okay. We're okay- everyone is okay, do not panic! Just thought I'd share some wisdom with you because the world around us has changed so much. You're pretty much the same though, just a little heavier, but that's a story for another time. Still childish, still impatient, and still empathetic as ever.

Growing up in a traditional Filipino household, there were only two feelings that were recognized by our parents. It was black and white; happy and mad. Thankfully, you know that there is a broad range of emotions that go beyond just happy and mad. I know being mad is not the opposite of being happy, but that's what our parents conveyed. You know this. They are not vulnerable with us and in return, it made us not vulnerable with them. What they put out we absorbed and emulated; same cynical cycle. Other feelings were non-existent so we hid the different feelings we felt because of this fact. We chose to be happy as a default feeling to avoid any conflict and misunderstandings.

Happiness was their goal from the beginning. Our parents came to America in search of that happiness for themselves and of course for their future children. It is the typical immigrant story and *our* story is no different. Our parents struggled putting a life together for us, but eventually came into jobs that were solid and stable. Our upbringing was common and we knew what was expected of us at an early age. I'm sure most Filipino families had their children's lives mapped out before they could even walk or talk. I wouldn't blame them though. That's what they thought would make us happy. They were projecting their happiness on us and I don't blame them for doing so. All they wanted was the best for us. Why am I talking about Mom and Pops? Don't worry, they're fine. They are living their best, retired lives! Again, the world around us has changed so much and I wanted to let you know that they have too. I know you think Mom and Pops are strict and set in their ways now, but over time, through a lot of conversations and ultimately life experiences, they've changed. They have changed for the better.

I bring this up because I know the resentment you feel towards them. After all, they were not able to communicate with you the way you hoped they would. The feelings you felt were repressed because of the inability of our parents to acknowledge those different feelings. The feelings you felt, currently feel, or will feel are valid. Read that again. You are allowed to feel any type of way towards anything and anyone. I know you lacked that validation growing up, so I am letting you know that it is more than okay and encouraged to feel more than happiness and anger. No one is mad at you for feeling all sorts of feelings. You wear your heart on your sleeve and always have; that is totally okay.

I hope this is getting through to you and you're not just rolling your eyes at this. This is important stuff! I need you to listen. Being different is okay. I know you know what I'm talking about. It's not just being able to communicate effectively with our parents. It is something scary, confusing, and unknown.

You are bisexual. Whether you've admitted it to yourself or not, you *are* and that is okay. Mom and Pops don't understand this concept yet, but they will. Oh boy, will they! Fast forward to today, you are in a loving, committed relationship with a one-of-a-kind woman. Your love is a once-in-a-lifetime love. You started as friends and with your charm, wit, and a bit of alcohol, she fell for you the way you fell for her so many years ago. She is definitely worth the wait, the effort, the time, and even the headaches. So all is good!

You'll go through some heartaches with both boys and girls and really have no one to share the experiences with because your feelings and identity are still repressed at this time. Keep on keeping on, Rana. Stay the course, focus, and you'll turn out great! I say this with gusto because I wouldn't want you to do anything different. Our life now is amazing! Although you didn't have our parents to comfort you with your heartaches, the lessons you learned by yourself strengthened who you are as a person. You raised yourself in many ways and you should be proud of that. Our parents tried their best. I'm not discrediting them for trying to raise us the way they did. I am empathetic to what they had to go through raising a bisexual daughter in a predominantly heterosexual Filipino world, especially in a country where sexual orientation is often criticized and misunderstood.

So this letter is not just for you, it's also for our parents. Please share this letter with Mom and Pops. The rest of this letter is for them just as much as it is for you to take in...

Hi Mom and Pops!

It's me! Your favorite firstborn- yes, Pops still makes that joke and we still pretend to chuckle to make the old man feel good. I'm coming to you from the year 2023. Sorry Pops, most of your hair is gone, but you're still a funny dude! Mom, you look really great still, a Forever21 auntie, but you don't dress like them- thank the Lord!

I just wanted to drop by and tell you how much I appreciate how you've both grown and changed over the past few years. I know right now it's scary and confusing, navigating a world where your daughter is deemed "different" by predetermined societal norms. Please take comfort in the fact that I am doing great and thriving in life! I know you're worried about me and how my life will play out because I'm bisexual. You can't help but be worried, I understand that.

I also understand that as scary as it was for me to come out it was probably just as scary for you and I never realized that until I got much older. I never considered your feelings because I was trying to figure out what this would all mean for me, myself and I. I am not apologizing for putting myself first, but I am recognizing that I could have been more understanding of your own broad range of emotions, Mom and Pops. I was caught up in my own feelings and in my own head that I never sat down and had a real conversation with you and how it would affect all of our lives. I know you'll say it didn't affect your lives, but I know it did. It hurt a handful of years and our relationship was strained because of it.

I know you tried to "pray the gay away." I know you tried to move me away from San Diego because you thought it was the environment. I know you had multiple conversations with your friends about this behind my back not realizing I was listening all along. The concerned, soft tones you spoke in, I will never forget. I know you tried to scare me straight, literally. I understand that you didn't have any guidance on being parents, even if Lolo and Lola were the best parents to you. It's different raising your own child because our personalities are different and no experiences are alike. The time and place you were raised in is far different from your world right now.

I do have to admit that it was a lot for me. I had to process all of these feelings on my own, but I'm here to tell you that I understand and that I wholeheartedly forgive you. For all of it. The lack of effective communication between us, the petty fights, the intimidation tactics, all the yelling, all of it. I forgive you for all of it because I know you were just trying to figure things out, too. I forgive you because I know you were just trying your best.

You wanted to be supportive after realizing and recognizing that it's not the end of the world to have a "different" daughter. You just didn't know how to communicate that. With all this talk about supporting the LGBTQIA+ community, the parents or parent figures also need support. I know that it's not about them and their lives, but we can't forget that they are also humans trying to figure things out.

There will be more resources than you can imagine to help guide you in all types of situations. Resources that can help you learn as individuals and learn as parents. Growth is inevitable whether you like it or not. And I'm thankful that we've all chosen to learn and grow together. Just take it one day at a time and reflect on what it means when you say you want your child to be happy. I promise you, everything will be just fine. Please keep learning and listening with an open mind. Our relationship will flourish and we'll be as close as ever.

One last thing, please absorb all that was said and apply it to your youngest daughter. If you thought I was a handful, just wait! Just kidding, she's great. She completes our family and the bond we all share is unlike anything in this world. It will be for years to come, trust me!

Thanks for taking in all of what I had to share, Mom and Pops. The rest is for my younger self.

Younger Rana, I know this was a lot for you; it was a lot for me too. If there is one thing I can leave you with, it's this: Give yourself grace *and* give our parents the same courtesy. You'll learn that seeking to understand someone else's perspectives while respecting them and practicing empathy are the best solutions to any situation you may face in life. You got this! I love you.

Always rooting for you,
Rana

WAG KA NANG MALUNGKOT - P. M.

Hoy,

Wag ka nang malungkot. Parati naman nagagalit si mom. Hindi lang niya nai-intindihan na mahusay ka sa pagkanta. Hindi niya alam na galing sa kanya ang kagandahang ginagaya mo. Paglaki mo, magagamit mo ang drag para ibahagi ang mga kwento ng mga Pilipina. Gagampanan mo ang mahahalagang papel ng ating mga magigiting na Pinay at ibabahagi mo ang kanilang mga pangarap kasama sa mga nakikibaka laban sa imperyalismo at kapitalismo. Sabi nga nila, huwag mo nang kahiligan ang arte, ngunit hindi nila alam na darating ang pana-hon na ikaw ay magiging kilala bilang si Maria Arte Susya Purisima Tolentino, di Ma. Arte for short. Ikaw ay makikilala sa paghahatid ng mga mahalagang laban sa pamamagitan ng, sa ingles, "dragging issues to the forefront." Tiisin mo ang hirap at kayang kaya mo ang lahat ng pagsubok.

XOXO,
P.M.

Don't Be Sad
English Translation

Hey,

Don't be sad. Mom is always angry. She just doesn't understand that you are good at singing. She doesn't know that the beauty you imitate comes from her. As you grow up, you will be able to use drag to share the stories of Filipinas. You will play an important role in sharing the dreams of our brave Pinays who are struggling against imperialism and capitalism. They say, don't fall in love with art, but they don't know that the time will come when you will be known as Maria Arte Susya Purisima Tolentino, or Ma. Arte for short. You will be known for delivering important battles, or in English, "dragging issues to the forefront." Endure hardship and you can handle all trials.

XOXO,
P.M.

20-Somethings - Ramon Alcantara

Dear 20-Something,

There's something you need to understand. Your parents wanted the best for you. They really did. They still really do. It must be frustrating to read this. You must hate it. You must not even want to continue reading this letter. Your pride must be boiling. You must be grinding your teeth. You must think the world is backward to know that your future self is even entertaining this idea.

I get it. I've lived it. I mean... You've lived it.

Your parents caused you pain whether or not they knew it and regardless of intent. To be honest, there will be days you wish that they would disappear. I know you have wished that you would disappear. To simply not exist. To never have existed at all. It's a shame you've even prayed for such a thing. Who made you feel this way? It was your parents. Your relatives. The company kept by your family. Your school. Your church. Your neighborhood. Society.

These evil feelings will make you face difficult decisions. You'll run away without barely saying a word. You'll change your phone number. You'll cut off contact to get away from your family; to get away from your parents. The funny thing is this. Every day you look in the mirror, you look more and more like your father. Oddly, on different days, you also see your mother's face staring back at you in your reflection. The truth is you really can't run away. Everywhere you go, there they are. As the years go by you'll notice the deep history in your face and realize you're a product of many generations before you.

Every wrinkle between your eyes, every gray hair on your head, and every gray hair on your chin will be reminders of time moving through you. They're reminders that time moves through your parents, who will be gone someday. They will be gone just like the generations before them.

The frustrating reality is that you are your parents' son. The permanent distance you've wished for will happen before you know it. The phone calls and texts you've been ignoring will someday stop coming. The option of having a conversation will someday be off the table. Will the next time you see them be the last?

At this moment, the present, they are alive and well. So let me share some history with you while I have your attention. You may not care to know this, but your parents came to the United States as 20-somethings in the 1980s. They were young, like you. Let's be honest, you at 20-something can barely read a map. Your mother and father had to travel to and navigate through a new world with limited resources and limited support. They had to build a new life with few friends and no family. They worked tirelessly as nurses to make money only to send it back to the Philippines where their parents and siblings were still living in impoverished communities.

Perhaps it was a burden to have a child, *you*, under such circumstances, but they did. That cannot be changed. So they did what they thought was best. They raised you in ways they thought was best. They certainly made mistakes along the way.

There are many ways they will disappoint you. They will not understand that their children are human beings with their own minds and souls. They will ignore *affection* to ensure *survival*. They will choose *sure and steady* over *adventure and joy*.

There are many ways you will disappoint them. You will take risks they were never brave enough to take. You will leave a woman to love a man. You will run away despite their genuine best efforts to love you.

We are all human. We all come from generations. In each generation, we learn to love and care differently and perhaps a bit better than generations before. But as humans, we are flawed. We may try our best, but we make mistakes and we grow. Just as you've learned from your mistakes, so have your parents. Please give them a chance. Please give them a call.

With Love,
Ramon

LESSON FIVE

Find your chosen family.

There is no doubt that the last chapter may have been a sore spot for some of you. It sure was for me. Still, I am blessed that I've reached a point in my life where it is crystal clear to me who is willing to show up for me and who will not. The vast majority of my relatives will stand by me and support me, and for that, I am immensely grateful and privileged. Over the years, my relationship with family was not without feelings of turmoil and shame, however.

The concept of family is interesting for Filipinos, isn't it? Being a *relative* is different from being *related* to Filipinos. Fictive kin is such a *thing* for Filipinos across the globe. To be honest, I can hardly keep track of who is truly related to me... by blood anyway. I grew up surrounded by other Filipinos who I viewed as uncles, aunts, and cousins because of their geographical proximity and constant presence in my everyday life. Even today, when I encounter Filipino elders or any parents or friends of color for that matter, my automatic reflex is to acknowledge them as *Tito*/Uncle or *Tita*/Auntie.

But what happens when people you view as family impart expectations that do not feel true to who you are?

What if I don't want children? What if I don't want to get married? What if I don't want to marry someone of a different gender? What if I don't even want to be in a romantic relationship with anyone at all?

These what-if scenarios come with so much pressure and stigma. Community is still so important to our survival as human beings. If our immediate family won't stand in our corner, we have to find a family who will.

I realize a lot of you who are reading this right now are dealing with traumas and challenges related to your family's feelings about your queerness. You may be in a period of transition with your immediate family members. Family should be there for you. They should support you. After all, they ought to know you best. This sadly isn't the case for many of us, and for that, I'd like to share a warranted reminder. If you're reading this book, there are people out there who do love you and will love you profoundly. These key individuals believe that if you are to experience the best parts of humanity in this short time you have on Earth, you must be afforded the opportunity to live authentically and in community with others.

As queer people who may have severed relationships with family members, many aspects of this book might make you feel emotions you are not ready to face, but if you've made it this far, consider leaning in; we're halfway to the end.

·♥·♥·♥·♥·♥·

In the United States and the Philippines, Filipino families often adhere to the tenets of *utang na loob* (debt of gratitude) and *hiya* (shame). These cultural norms of internalized debt and shame are for the benefit of the collective group. Strengthening familial relationships and collective approaches were survival mechanisms for Filipinos who were especially newer to the United States. For example, according to Almirol (1982), the dependence and loyalty that Filipino farm and domestic laborers had for one another during the 1920s and 1930s were necessary to ensure their safety and security as a group.

The concept of *utang na loob* refers to a perpetual feeling of an internal debt that might never be repaid. It has its purpose; *utang na loob*, ensures that family members act and give in ways that benefit others as well as the whole family unit before the needs and desires of the self. To act in ways that put the self above the family or in conflict with familial expectations is to be *walang hiya* (shameless), which has tremendously negative connotations. "Have you no shame?"

Again, coming out as queer Filipinos might be seen as a selfish move by parents and family members who adhere to *utang na loob*. To be queer, doesn't immediately benefit others. In fact, it triggers emotions such as fear; fear of perhaps disrupting the family lineage. Thus, it puts the queer individual in a position to be labeled as *walang hiya*.

But we are human. To be made to feel like we must have shame for who we are hurts the soul. Everyone wants what's best for everyone, but at least in the beginning for queer Filipino Americans, the path to how this can happen is rocky. The differences in expectations among queer Filipinos and their family members will cause conflicts that sooner or later pull the family unit apart.

·♥·♥·♥·♥·♥·

The letters featured in this chapter were selected because the content of each one reflects an expressed need to belong. Some letters discuss community and a sense of belonging as general concepts. Others describe specific formal organizations and affinity groups to which they belong because of shared interests. And the rest talk about deeply valued friendships and non-romantic relationships.

Human beings are social creatures and having a sense of belonging is considered by many to be a basic human need. Having a sense of belonging is linked to many positive outcomes in physical and mental health, as well as general well-being (Haim-Kitevsky et al., 2023). For Filipinos, this shared ethnic identity is what binds us together. This *kapwa* (togetherness) that we feel is a desire to be connected simply because we are Filipino.

When the family units we're born into do not claim us because of our queerness, we lose out on this sense of belonging that everyone so desperately craves. For queer people, we turn to our chosen family to fill this need. Chosen family refers to the core group of individuals who fulfill those loving and supportive roles that might be traditionally filled by a parent or sibling. The great thing about a chosen family is not necessarily that we *need* one another (although it's true), but that we show up for one another because we *want* to show up for one another. We recognize the inherent value in the humanity of our chosen family members. We don't show up for one another out of obligation per se. We show up for one another out of mutual love, passion, respect, and care.

DANCE AS IF EVERYONE IS WATCHING - DR. ARNEL CALVARIO RIPKENS

Dear 10-Year-Old Arnel Calvario,

There is something deep within yourself that feels different.

Being picked last whenever people made teams for basketball or football in your neighborhood hurt you and created deep fears of rejection.

Being called "sissy" or "weird" mortified you into toning yourself down when you really deserved to shine your truth so brightly.

However, at the park and at the parties, you found freedom & community through Hip Hop dance.

You learned teamwork, discipline, pride in your Fil-Am heritage, and the power of performance quality when you performed Filipino cultural dances with your cousins.

Although not valued in all the spaces you will enter, lean into your love for DANCE.
Lean into your curiosity, creativity, and communal mindset.

Give value to your time with those who include & uplift you vs. giving power to those who ostracize & judge you.

That something different inside YOU is special.

One day, the more you lean into what makes you extraordinary,
the greater you will feel & know your unique purpose
and the great impact it can make in the world.

Who YOU ARE MATTERS.
Who YOU ARE is deserving of not only acceptance,
but of LOVE & CELEBRATION.

So go out there and dance as if EVERYONE is watching.

Your future best friend,
50 Year-Old Dr. Arnel Calvario Ripkens

To Love Oneself - Gabe Sagisi

Dear Gabe,

How are you? I know...that must be a loaded question.

It must be exciting for you; being a social butterfly with a bunch of positivity, ambitious to make his mark on the world, working toward being recognized as a Filipinx American leader, and uplifting his community in every way he can...and yet, you're holding so much on your mind.

Ever since middle school, you retreated to extracurriculars, academic course-work, and any excuse to keep yourself from going home. You thought home was a place where you felt safe and secure, and where you could recover from your arduous days. But, you found that going home forced you to deal with generational trauma and unravel yourself to your family. You've come face-to-face with all the things you're not, what you could do better, and how, in some cases, you've already failed.

Lacking a truly safe space with family developed ongoing trauma that even seeped into your career endeavors, authenticity, and overall spirit as a human being. There were days when you even questioned if you'd see tomorrow.

Our culture often emphasizes that "family is everything," but know that you can also lean on family that you aren't necessarily related to. You've established meaningful connections with friends across the U.S. and made a chosen family of those who understand you best. These members of your inner circle have seen you overcome hardship, seen you grow, and empowered you through the valleys that life takes you through.

Their love and support helped push you to take a leap of faith and do the best thing you could ever do for yourself, which was moving across the country to start anew. Through this, you were able to heal, come to terms with a lot of your past, and see yourself in a different light that could not shine enough until you stepped out of what you were already naturally exposed to.

As you've learned with age, many environments will often hold you back from seeing your truest, authentic self. At the end of the day, being queer is coming to terms with what is and isn't sustaining you in this lifetime. We are survivors and have to fight every day for our existence to resonate within our communities.

In a world that will punish you, degrade you, and even try to make the case that you don't deserve to be here, know that <u>You</u> have proven that you can change your life for the better, fought when the world kept pushing you down, and, of course, exemplified what it looks like to thrive in spaces that aren't built for queer Filipinx Americans.

And in the roughest of moments you face, please know, as always, that love starts and ends with you.

Yours Truly,
Gabe

Gumagalang Magmula Sa Puso - elle Zulueta

Hey kid,

Oh man, have I wanted to talk to you. You were right; you made the right decision to hold on. Spoilers: Life is so much better than you could have possibly imagined; so let's take it from the top.

Remember how much you loved/hated the phrase, *I'm not like other girls*? How it felt so pretentious, but resonate so strongly with you? Because you were right! You aren't like other girls because you are non-binary!! You've known it in your heart since elementary school, but don't really know the term until college. Gender was never something you wanted to adhere to; you always found yourself wanting to do something. Not because it was masculine or feminine, but because it was something you wanted to do. And guess what, you still do! You find out that even though the world as a whole doesn't fully understand this concept, you find people who are willing to learn. Some of them are already with you, so keep them close.

You move out, which gives you the freedom you longed for, for so long. I know Ma and Pa were strict growing up, but the separation helps, and everything mellows out between us. Hell, you tell them that you're non-binary which was our milestone for being openly non-binary to the world. Ma was the more vocal one when we came out saying, "No matter how you identify yourself is up to you and we still love you." However, Pa is more accepting and supportive. He remembers to say "anak" instead, and comforts us when we have to stand our ground as a non-binary person. They're better, but I still keep my distance. It's mainly because we're busy with something that becomes near and dear to your heart.

You will eventually join a martial arts academy: Filipino Kali Academy (FKA) in Norwood, NJ. We literally did not think much of it. You get into volleyball during COVID (yeah, that's a whole can of worms, that's for another time), and play pick-up games in Prospect Park in Brooklyn. However, when it got too cold to play volleyball outside, you wanted to stay active, so you Googled a place to do "that Filipino double stick martial art". We kind of got lazy about it, but decided to go because they had a Labor Day sale going on. And like most things, we were so shy about it. We didn't know how we wanted to present ourselves, we didn't know how to introduce ourselves. Especially since we wouldn't know how they would accept someone who's non-binary because, let's face it, these sorts of spaces aren't very accepting of "others." But to your surprise, Master Ace

Ramirez, the head instructor of the academy, gives a speech during class about comfort zones and how to get to second base, you have to leave the security of first. It resonated so much with you since you were racking your brain about it for a whole week, and he talked as if he was aware. You tell him right after class about your identity. We were so nervous, we wanted to bail out so badly, but he was so accepting to the point that he offered to tell the other coaches for us. They take a bit to adjust to it, (we understand for a lot of people that it takes a bit of rewiring) but they eventually do, and it feels so affirming every time.

There's a phrase that we say before and after every class, "Gumagalang magmula sa puso", which means, "With respect, from the heart." We find it funny because Pa always preached about doing stuff "from the heart" all the time, yet here we are. So far away from home but we still see this. Here, however, it feels more genuine than when we heard it growing up. In every other group we were in: volleyball, yoga, DT, etc., we just showed up. We didn't interact too much with anyone, especially outside the time slots. But everyone is so friendly, perceptive, and supportive of you in FKA, that you want to return that sentiment. You break out of your shell, you interact with your fellow students both on and off the mat, hell, you teach children Kali! And you have fun with it!! After roughly 2 years in FKA, one of your Kali friends talks to you about your Kali journey: Being this shy individual that he wasn't sure was going to stick around with one of the higher-ranking people in the academy. He mentioned how when we got our first hearty laugh during one of the classes, he knew that we were going to stay. We were surprised that anyone was paying attention to us and how we operated. I certainly didn't notice. There was one thing that we would notice about ourselves during training: How much we smile. We have so much fun, it's something we love to do. It brings us so much happiness, through the training and through the community, and it has never felt so good.

It was a long journey, but you do find yourself, you do find your people, and you do find your passion. Just stick around, it truly is worth it.

Gumagalang magmula sa puso!
elle

Between the Lines - Gabriella Buba

Dear Younger Me,

It's hard to be different. To be between. To look like no one you know on the outside, and feel like no one you know on the inside. They say you have your father's nose. Grandma means this as a compliment as she pinches and pinches the flat bridge of your sister's button nose, trying to form a bridge. You cry anyway. Your skin is too dark. Your hair, too unruly. You have a horse face. She means this with love. "You would be so beautiful if only—"

You wish you were beautiful like she is and was. Your sister is a perfect carbon copy of your mother, and she of your grandmother. Pong. Three of a kind, clicking neatly as mahjong tiles. What one feels the other knows. They are in sync, in tune, dancing to music only they hear, and you are outside of it.

You are awkward and mannish, and not quite entirely of your father or your mother. What are you? People will guess. They will be wrong. Exotic. Foreign. Strange.

You will try to explain your roots and how you have grown the way you have, but they are not listening. You will try to explain the *not-like-other girls* feeling that is growing inside you, the confusing crushes, the heart-pounding fear. They are not listening.

But you will find your people. It will take time. You will grow into your limbs, and your unruly curls, your horse face, and nose. Your confusing crushes and the heart pounding, you will discover, is not fear. You will paint your nails red, and while julienning carrots for pancit, you will see your mother and your grandmother's hands in your own at last. You will belong in pieces, but you will belong.

With Love,
Gabriella Buba

The One to Be for the Ones Who Need - Harlee Castro Balajadia

To the one who wished there was someone for them,

In your day and age, being a Brown, Gay, 1st-Gen, Thicc, Outspoken, Filipino Boy was to be the most outcast of outcasts. The hardest part was knowing this and yet everyone around you only knew how to comment and retort without seeking to understand how you must have felt inside. Especially back then, the US was RUTHLESS on anyone who wasn't the American Dream. I know you may not feel it right now, but in this day and age, you are the dream of where so many other people are striving to be. And I know that it's also looked down upon to self-edify and try to give yourself appreciation – but really. It's amazing to see that the person you've become today, has been a result of your journey of finding someone you needed.

Just letting you know... you're living the dream. You're a full-time music teacher and a full-time musician. You've always dreamt of being able to do both (because let's be honest with each other – you're greedy and always want to do everything), but because of that passionate hunger, you're there. Your impact on the world? It's vastly wider than you thought you'd ever have. To be able to be the adult you are now has become a beacon for your students, friends, colleagues, and family. You've been able to influence the spirit of people because of the person you're choosing to be.

Do you want to know why it's so effective? Because you've committed to being the one person you needed for yourself. You've promised to be the one that so many other people needed, both back then and right now. You know that when your students leave the classroom, they are equipped with everything you wish you had growing up. That's really freaking cool to see that all of the hard work you've put into navigating through this world, it's packed into one person who's literally influencing the next generation. It's cliche to say that there's only ever one of you – because we all know that every person is unique in their own way. But it's important to remember that we're all human and we all share similar experiences of life. But because you're braving through the world to be the person you are, you're shining a light for others to lead the way. Keep on shining on.

With Love,
Your Thriving Current Self

Letting People In - Dr. Michelle Fortunado-Kewin

Dear Meesh,

Hello beautiful
I hope you recognize me
It's October 2023
It's Filipino American History Month and
LGBTQ+ History Month
You've just entered the final year of your 30s

Your childhood was fine
Your teen years were rough
And adulthood had its ups and downs
But you made it
You're still HERE
You're not only surviving but you're thriving

Let's go back to the start
Daly City has been and will always be "home"
You've always been surrounded by Filipino people...
...at home, at school, at the grocery store, and of course, at the mall
But school forced you to assimilate into being "American"

You lost your native tongue
You struggled with being "darker" than others
Your weight was up and down
You never felt "smart" enough, "cool" enough, "beautiful" enough
You constantly compared yourself to your Filipino friends and cousins
You struggled to figure out who you are

You tried taking science and math classes to become a nurse
But your heart wasn't there
Your parents supported you
But they had difficulty guiding you as immigrants who didn't understand the
American school system

You were an average student
But you made it through
You even got a scholarship
You went to college

Got a bachelor's degree
And guess what...you even got a master's and doctorate degree

There was something about college where you started feeling free
You started going to therapy
You started exploring your identity
It wasn't until your late 20s
After tons of learning and unlearning about what it means to be
Filipino-American
That you realized that there were parts of you that you were suppressing

Friends, colleagues, clients, and so many others shared their coming out process
with you
You've always held space for others when they shared this intimate part of their
identity
You validated them, honored them, and loved them for who they were,
regardless of who they loved or how they identified

A colleague shared an experience about what being queer meant
And instead of "coming out"
They described this beautiful process of "letting people in"
What if...instead of "coming out"
You "let people in"
How freeing would that be

Over the past 10 years, you've slowly let people in
It hasn't been an easy or comfortable process
And you've struggled with the terminology around queer identity
What does it all mean?
Are you queer? Bi? Pan?
It's pretty fluid but queer and bi is what you typically use

Everyone you've "let in" over the past years has loved, held, and supported you
It's still a slow process
And not everyone in your family or inner circle knows this
But that's okay
Just take your time and just breathe.

You're beautiful
You're loved
You're seen
And now you're free to just be

> With Love,
> Dr. Meesh

So Many Families - P. M.

Hey,

It's me again. Checking in. You've been down about family for a while. I know being queer, we become disconnected for our own self-preservation. You think if you'll ever have a family of your own. Well, let's imagine a more expansive idea of family. You will be part of so many types of families. Those friends from high school, the ones in the arts, will still be there for you. Especially that Pinay cheerleader! You share memes and messages about how our other friends have kids, while we vacation around the world. You both check in with one another and support each other when our parents continue to parent us with shame and disappointment. We start to forgive our parents a bit and try to understand how much hurt they continue to endure because they continue to invest in this toxic American dream. In the military-industrial complex. In white supremacy. In anti-blackness. In xenophobia. In classism. In cisheteropatriarchy. In the name of the Father, the Son, and the Holy Spirit.

You'll have so many families! The bestie in West Virginia with his Black Panamanian husband takes you in at the end of November. Wild and wonderful. Queers in Appalachia baking croissants and *alfajores*. Nomada en Huntington. The Pinoys in the Prairies. They sustained you while you trained for the hardest journey you had so far -- a Ph.D. degree. This group of Filipino/Americans found each other on stolen and dispossessed land of the Peoria, Kaskaskia, Peankashaw, Wea, Miami, Mascoutin, Odawa, Sauk, Mesquaki, Kickapoo, Potawatomi, Ojibwe, and Chickasaw Nations. They will shelter you; they will feed you. One will break your heart in a million pieces and you still love him even though he no longer feels the same way.

So many families! Like your children. Not the biological result of gametes joining, but of sharing a learning space. The space of a classroom births justice and liberation out of our discouraged minds that move joy, care, admiration, and pride from our hearts. You watch them graduate and prepare them to be better people in the world. Like last night, you helped two Filipina students in Wiyot land host a potluck for Filipinx/a/o American History Month at the university where you are a professor. You made too much food. You stayed up late the night before to make chicken adobo and a mushroom version for the vegetarians. Then a deconstructed pancit bihon so people who don't eat pork can choose the sauteed chicken or the Chinese-style sweet sausage. You felt bad that you didn't have time to make the shitake version for the vegetarians.

Remember the joy from karaoke to Disney songs, NSYNC, and the Otso Otso. The mixed-raced Black Filipina, Black White, Black Latine, the new immigrant Filipina from Cagayan De Oro, the new Pinay colleague at the local community college eating dishes our moms taught us. So many families! And you will appreciate our family too. It's an ongoing process.

So many families to nourish your soul. Keep it up.

I love you so much even if it's so difficult to hear.

P.M.

I Refuse to Stop Dreaming - Warjay Naigan

To You, 18 Years Ago

You've lived through so much; so much for a child. You've experienced agony in ways no human being should experience. Yet peers, adults, and the system have failed you.

You've been through so much, and it's not your fault. You are not the unwanted fruit to be discarded. You are born into a heinous system active in rooting out the most beautiful and gentle aspects of this world.

Nevertheless, between then and now your story continues to fill.

At certain points, you've kept yourself from the world, choosing to view it atop the vast expanse of your computer screen. You've learned, imperfectly, to attempt to love what stands before you in the mirror. But you believe that love can only ever come from yourself. You lose faith in humanity, yet I know you yearn for belonging. You yearn to trust again. I do not blame you for believing this, you did what you had to to survive.

In other moments, you rend and rip yourself apart, trying to reshape into a space that never wanted you as you to begin with. You come to hate and cringe at yourself, denying the pieces of you that you worked so hard to love for the hollow sense of community that could never fathom the depth of your soul. And again, I tell you that I do not blame you for believing this, you did what you had to do to survive.

The system has always told you to choose, to be realistic about what was possible. But I refuse to stop dreaming of my future into existence. I dream of a better world, and a community capable of loving me because I am me. Full stop.

We find community. Small, yet precious; we find a community that helps to heal wounds they didn't even cause. Remember this letter when you eventually hear the line from a powerful song, "I know I'm quite the catch, but why fake it all just to be loved back."

At the time of writing this, I cannot claim to have healed from the pain of our past. But I want to try. And I do try; we try. Every day we tap into an unbridled joy and tenderness found in the depths of our childhood. And we try our best to let that feeling guide our path forward.

The world is wide and vast, beyond the boundaries laid out for you by systems and people who don't take the time to know you.

You're not a line in the story of the world, you're the whole fucking book.

And with that, I have one request: Please stay.

Peace,
Warjay

LESSON SIX

BREAK A FEW RULES AND HAVE FUN.

When I was in kindergarten, I distinctly remember having conversations with my mother about Heaven and Hell. To be honest, my most memorable conversations about religion with my mother revolved around the concept of Hell. I imagine her goal was specifically to impart the importance of behaving in ways that would ensure I would avoid *that place*. I imagined Hell to be red like the pictures of Mars in science books and full of volcanoes that were perpetually erupting into black skies.

We had a bulletin board on the wall next to our landline phone, which we used primarily to pin phone numbers, notes, and a yearly calendar. My mother posted a Heaven and Hell chart to this bulletin board to track my behaviors. It was a simple and (temporarily) effective strategy that scared me into doing as I was told. The chart was a white sheet of computer paper with a line drawn down the middle to make two columns. *Heaven* (for tracking obedient behaviors) on one side, and *Hell* (for tracking disobedient behaviors) on the other. Occasionally, when I was behaving like a *good* child, she'd add a tally mark in the Heaven column. If ever I was on the brink of a tantrum, or if I didn't follow a precise instruction, my mother would walk me over to the bulletin board so that I could watch her add a tally mark on the Hell side. Each tally mark, she explained, represented taking one step closer to either Heaven or Hell. And of course, if I was being a disobedient child, I'd find myself walking closer and closer to the fiery pits of Hell. For good measure, with every tally mark in the Hell column, she'd make an off-hand comment that she could see horns growing from my forehead, implying I was slowly turning into a literal devil monster. It terrified me into having nightmares of being in Hell and running away from walls of fire.

Honestly, I tell this story to close friends from time to time to give them a laugh about what my life was like growing up. I will also go on record to say that my mother is a very nice lady who loves me dearly. Still, this story is a close representation of how it felt for me and perhaps for other queer Filipinos who grew up in religious households or communities. There are rules to follow and the right way to be *good*.

My hindsight tells me those conversations with Mom were more so about scaring me into obedience. In the way that I reminisce and laugh about ridiculous childhood memories, I tell friends about this specific instance in which religion was used in my house to get *good* behavior from us children.

Though this strategy used might be unique to my mother, the sentiment holds true. Fostering this fear of being labeled as *bad* or *deviant* has a purpose. This fear of being sent straight to Hell has a purpose.

Obedience.

Blind obedience for that matter. A parental figure, an adult, or any authority figure may encourage blind obedience because it's the easy approach to creating order. In some cases, fostering fear specifically is an easy approach to gaining power.

·♥·♥·♥·♥·♥·

The intersectionality of being queer and Filipino in the United States means we are part of multiple oppressed identities. Queer folks are marginalized because they fall outside the norms of the gender binary and/or heterosexuality. Filipino Americans have a unique racialized experience in the United States. We are neither seen as fully American due to being people of color or being of Asian descent, yet we are also not always racialized as Asian. Dr. Anthony Ocampo (2016) explores this concept more fully in his book, *The Latinos of Asia*; he states that due to Filipinos' phenotypical characteristics in addition to our people's history of Spanish colonization, we are culturally and observably similar to Latinos. Of course, we are a distinct people as Filipinos. And as queer people, we have identities that are not quite understood nor accepted by the masses. So the perceptions of us queer Filipinos held by the dominant culture continue to push us into proverbial boxes.

Well I don't know about you all, but I personally don't want to be pushed into a box; I would rather have some control over my own life. When we are blindly obedient to the rules that are created by the dominant culture, we are at risk of surrendering our sense of control, our sense of agency, and our bodily autonomy. The rules we live by are in place to maintain social order. The thing about rules is that we ought to be critical of them. Rules ought to change over time. When society changes, rules ought to change too.

·♥·♥·♥·♥·♥·

For many queer Filipinos, we are pushed into a box made of strict rules and expectations when we're young. We're made to think the box is our whole lives. We must operate within the box. There is nothing beyond the box. But then suddenly, something happens. You see a light come through a crack in the box. You get a taste of what's outside the box. You take a peek outside the box and you realize that the world is so much bigger than you were told to imagine.

The letters that are featured in this section explore the concept of rules and constraints. Specifically, the writers express how playfully defying the norms and expectations placed on them as queer Filipinos isn't so bad. You have a right to explore outside the box. You'll have a good time outside of the box. Playful exploration in the areas of life that are scary gives you the courage to be more of who you are and to discover more of what feels right to you. Break a few rules; you'll have fun. I promise.

RIGHT NOW AND FOREVER - HARLEE CASTRO BALAJADIA

If I could tell you just one thing...

It's that I'm so proud that you've created such a loving and grounding relationship with yourself.

I'm sure you're already listing in your brain all of the people to thank who have helped remind and empower you to have a relationship with yourself. Don't worry - they know that you're grateful for them. They can feel it. They can sense it. They can feel it. And you want to know how?

You're standing and living in this moment - writing this letter right now and reading it in your mind.

You don't even know how many other people are reading this letter in their lives knowing that because you're living today - they have the courage to do the same.

Thank you for giving me the time and space to be with yourself. Thank you for trusting in yourself. Thank you for knowing that the relationship you have with you is the most important relationship. Thank you for loving yourself as much as you love other people - for all the people you want to be grateful for. It's not just pouring into our own cup. It's not just filling our own cup. It's switching out the cup of ourselves and breaking the mold and becoming a bowl. Becoming a vessel of love that not only allows others to pour into us, but allows the same level of greatness to share and commune with others around us. To share this sense of love and importance amongst people. To realize that we don't just have to be a cup - but we can be a fountain of love for others.

It's awesome to see how happy you've become enjoying your own company. To see how you never wanted to be alone, but now - your kindred spirit allows so many people to uncover the biases of alone time, and rewrite their assumptions about life into a narrative that supports them.

With Love,
Your Proud Self of Today

FLAMBOYANT - FRANCIS JOSEPH J. GALLEGO

Skinny and with a big ass head,

Those fucking bullies called you flamboyant and you didn't know what it meant. I also remember you being 5 or 6; being called a fag for the first time and asking your white grandpa what it meant. He said it was cigarettes.

I know that you continue to hide in the libraries and beg your mom to take you to school hella early because you don't want to deal with those cruel bullies. I also know that you have no one to talk to, and you are ashamed. Please know that these moments will build you, but don't make it harden you. Continue to be your authentic and kind self, and ignore those bullies who told you who you were before you even knew. Even though they have tried to steal your joy, they can never take your spirit.

It's okay to play Miss Universe with your cousins; pretending to have long hair with towels, wearing grandma's shoes and comforters for evening gowns. Fantasies make you dream. I know that it is so hard to deal with the disappointment of your family, but I know you know your grandma loves you so much. Please know that you don't ever need to beg for love. Your grandma's unconditional love will make you survive all of this.

You will not die alone, and I know that AIDS is scary, but do not succumb to the stigma of it. There are so many lost generations of so many queer brothers who died of AIDS and shared trauma, but remember your queerness is an act of resistance.

You are a flamboyant queen.

Dance,
Francis

BAHALA NA: A LETTER TO ACCEPT AND UNDERSTAND - AV AUDVISION

Dear AV,

If I asked you to be clear with your intentions with who you love and how you love, what would you say? Your family, your partner, and close friends? Would you list your results for love languages or say your non-negotiables? Lately, I have been exploring that when I answer these questions I say the usual: Friends, Family, Partners, Acts of Service, Affirmations, and A LOT of affection. Then I move forward but then recognize I forget to extend the love I want from others to also be for myself.

My love has always been strong, expressive, and in some moments redirected in efforts that leave my reservations for my own wants to run dry. How do I combat this? I have been handwriting letters to comfort myself whenever I wanted or needed someone else to do so for me. Does it feel lonely? Absolutely. Does it work for me? Most definitely. Here is the letter I wrote to myself on a day when I needed the love I wanted from others:

> *Dear A******,*
> *As a kid you found "joy" escaping into letters you wrote when you were feeling blue while waiting for the walls to just...close. Today 28, feeling the emptiness fill the room, you stop and think. You accept your fate. You do not know the future. You have to accept the past and do better in the present. If the younger you knew it got better the next day you would have seen an opportunity to believe in yourself when all else failed. Believe in yourself. Love YOU the way you have tried to love others. Use what you know as strengths and be aware of what others see as weaknesses. Be true and honest with yourself and your mistakes. Honor your life's worth by simply looking at how much you've done to live.*

I love you AV. Please be kind to yourself.

Sincerely,
AV

BABY HAZE - HAZEL BONDOC CARRANZA

Dear Baby Haze,

"Girl, boy, *bakla*, tomboy, *butiki*, *baboy* (girl, boy, gay, tomboy/lesbian, lizard, pig)" — have you found out which one you are from that Filipino children's rhyme?

You had always looked one way and felt another; but never any of the following words after "girl" – except for "baboy" or "pig" due to being overweight and being called it growing up.

There were so many blockages for you to see yourself clearly.
Cultures within cultures, differences among differences, relationship after relationship.
You've had to look into each and every door to find yourself.
Good news is, you finally got it, love! Or at least a pathway to more understanding.

You were always scared to be seen in any way other than "girl" that you felt like it was okay to hide your rich and sultry alto voice. Your first church choir only knew you as a soprano. They missed a completely different range and side of you. And so did you.

Growing up with "older girls" who plucked and got glammed up on one side of the family, then with ones who kept it simple on the other must have kept you on a roller coaster ride of sorts.

Top that off with always being given "girly" clothes as gifts and not having enough money to buy your own. Clothes are a big part of someone's identity. Unfortunately, you didn't have the time or space to explore for a while... You would never have even had to face the confusion that you could be attracted to girls too, until you got jealous over a "friend" having less and less time for you. Or maybe you had an inkling when you liked an all-out masculine-presenting "tomboy" clown at a family party when you were about 10-years-old? You were never nearly girly enough nor tomboy enough, so no one knew there was even a slight struggle. You look like a "girl," all the way.

You would have hated being called a tomboy too, even though you were always your grandfather's favorite, and you wanted to be more like him. Gentle, strong, kind – you loved him enough that you wanted to make sure you learned how to whistle songs just like he did, and bust ballroom dancing moves that made Lola's heart flutter every night. Girl or tomboy, you knew you were a romantic!

Forgive me if the words are not completely correct, as this is the first time I am telling anyone this. You never had to pick one, you only had to pick yourself.

By not wanting to just be "girl," or "tomboy," we found out that we didn't lack anything being either, both, or neither of those words. We are who we are and that is enough. We have always been enough just as we are.

We do end up marrying a wonderful cisgender male, a masculine-presenting partner who loves the crap out of us, though.

The only way that we would have found our fully embodied self was always with lots of love, and we have finally found the safest space to be able to love the version of us that we see in the mirror– fully, completely, and without hesitation. I have finally found love within myself.

So moving forward in this journey I open myself to even more.

With Love,
Tita Celing

PS: Here's a song I wrote just for you and how all sorts of love had felt for you in all the parts of your searching, up until today.

This is called, "Kahit Minsan Lang" or "Just Take a Moment" by Hazel B. Carranza.

Kahit Minsan Lang

Madalas akong umuuwi ng luhaan
Iyak ng iyak
Di na malaman kung sa'n sisimulan
Mga kwento ng pag-iwan
Salaysay ng kanilang paglisan

Lagi na lang akong sawi at sugatan
Hindi ba nila alam na ang alay ko'y walang hanggan?

Kahit minsan lang, kahit minsan lang
Sumilip man lang sakin
Pakinggan aking damdamin
Kahit minsan lang, kahit minsan lang

Ibigin lang ako iingatan ko ang puso mo

Naiisip man lang kaya nila ako
Isang babaeng handang ibigay ang lahat
Pati ang mundo
Kailanman di na umahon
Sa hapdi lagi naman bumabangon

Hindi ba nila alam
'Di ako ang nawawalan
Dahil 'pag ako ang nagmahal
Tiyak na magpakailanman

Nandito lang ako
Naghihintay kahit kailan sa'yo
At kahit na 'di mo 'ko mapansin
Dinggin mo lang ang aking damdamin
Ito'y damhin

· ♥ · ♥ · ♥ · ♥ · ♥ ·

Just Take A Moment
English Translation

I mostly come home in tears
Constantly crying
Not knowing where to start
The stories of how I lost them
Narratives of how I felt when they've let go

I'm always left unlucky and bleeding
Don't they know that what I offer is forever?

Just take a moment, just take a moment
Take a good look at me
Listen to my heart
Just take a moment, just take a moment
Love me and I'll take care of your heart

Do they even think about me
Someone willing to give their everything

Including the world
I couldn't ever come up for a breath
And still, I got up with every lash on my body

Don't they know
That this is not my loss
Because when it's me who loves
It's meant to be forever

I'm just here
Waiting for forever for you
And even if you may never see me
Can you at least hear what my heart has to say?
Will you feel it?

Hoy, Love Yourself! - Mara De La Rosa

Dear Sweet Nine-Year-Old Baby Mara,

Don't be scared, it's you! From the future. Haha. This is pretty crazy, right? It's been a year since you moved here, how's America treating you so far?? Just kidding, I know it's been tough. And it feels like things will always be miserable, but that's so far from the truth! Things get better.

Guess what, you're super gay! I know that you know and I know that it's scary, but girl, let me tell you there's nothing to be scared about. I'm actually here to give you some advice, *lez girl* to *lez girl*.

Remember Sister Josephine from Father Angelico Lipani school in Las Piñas? Our first-ever girl crush? And Honey, our neighbor? If I recall correctly Honey's boy cousin Marc had a crush on us and the whole block was so *kinikilig, thrilled*. Except us. Remember how it felt like you were having an out-of-body experience and being paired with Marc *never* felt right? And how you told our cousin, Ate PR, about Honey being your crush and she stared back at you with eyes so wide you thought her eyeballs were going to fall out?

You were already so open about your sexuality then; remember that. The "wrongs" of being gay were taught to you by society–it doesn't mean what they say is right. I encourage you to live life fully as YOURSELF. Never apologize. Be the fun, gay, and free version of Mara. She's the best.

Right now, it's the early 2000s and people, especially kids, are still unwelcoming towards the LGBTQ community. Plus you just moved from the Philippines, so you're still trying to navigate life in America. It seems so awful, but don't worry, it's all character-building for you. It helps you, us, become stronger and more independent. The bullies are just hurt people trying to hurt people. But hear me out, I have some helpful advice to share with you.

Mom.
Mom isn't going to be super accepting–at first! Give her time, you're her baby. She's a baby boomer and they were taught that being gay is a sin. She really, really, really times infinity loves you, but she has to go through her own emotions. We all do. Eventually, she becomes such a big supporter of your queerness and even encourages you to go on dates! She is literally the best and most supportive mother in the world.

Go to therapy.
Honestly if anything, ask Mom if you can go sooner. Reassure her it's normal.
If she doesn't budge, start screaming and crying and throwing things. Freak her
out and then ask to go to therapy, it works. Oh, and therapy DOES NOT go on
your "record," tell her that. There are no records, everyone needs therapy, that's
a fact.

Practice meditation, I know you think it's silly and maybe a little scary, but this
will really help with your future anxieties and mental health.

Coming-out story at Sushi Stop.
Make sure to cry really hard when you tell your future best friends, Kari and
Mari, about your coming-out story at Sushi Stop in Hollywood. I repeat; really
feel your feelings because someone WILL feel so bad for you that they end up
paying for dinner. We'll need that free dinner!

Career tips.
Go to school for coding or engineering, really anything in tech. You will be
thankful for it. You can still pursue your dream career; you'll just do it more
comfortably. That or invent a social media application called "Instagram," or
"Facebook."

Sorry, I know I'm digressing, but I just want the best for you/us!

Everyone is on the queer spectrum.
I wholeheartedly believe that everyone is on the queer spectrum. In sophomore
year of high school, you'll learn in Biology class that all women are born bisexual,
and baby you are litty for the titty and the clitty.

I know I sound crazy promiscuous and probably too excited, but I need you to
get here SOONER.

LOVE YOURSELF!

Come out in High School.
Everyone already knows you're gay and they're going to be talking about it
behind your back, so why not talk about it in front of your back? Face to face?
Proudly! Own it. Who cares what other people think?

Our family moved here for the *American Dream*, so live it up. You're here, living
in a first-world country, there's cold and warm water in the shower. Let loose!

Girl Crushes.
There's going to be this girl you act within the musical *Chicago*! The Velma
to your Mama Morton. You'll look at her and butterflies will flutter in your
stomach. GO FOR IT. She's gay!!! Things didn't really happen between you
two, but if you go for it, oooh weee, things *could* happen.

Don't take anything too personally. People act the way they do because they're
going through so much of their own shit.

Be fully queer in College!
Join the GSA club at your school.

Write queer characters in your plays. You don't need to make the characters
straight!

Start asking people out, get used to rejection sooner.

In college, your friend PAs for Paramount and she'll offer to take you around
the studio, and you'll bring a girl with you, let's call her Marilyn. You'll wear
a really cute outfit and so will Marilyn, and y'all will have dinner and drive by
the *American Horror Story* house (it's a TV show). Afterward, Marilyn will ask
you to come into her apartment, but you'll be so focused on your damn thesis and writing the valedictorian speech. GIRL! GO. INSIDE. MARILYN'S.
APARTMENT. YOU'RE NOT VALEDICTORIAN AND THAT THESIS
DOESN'T DEFINE YOU!

Come out to the rest of the family.
Eventually, you'll come out to your cousins and everyone is super supportive.
The *Titos/Titas* are supportive online, but due to cultural and age differences,
it's not really something we talk about. But I encourage you to keep pushing
through that glass ceiling. The fact that Mom is as open as she is now is so cool.

Also, so many women in our family are gay. I'll let you figure out who they are
when the time comes, it's a funner reveal that way. And possibly one boy gay
cousin, though I can't confirm because we're not that close.

Heartache.
We're going to experience a lot of heartache in life, and trauma, but I don't
want you to be afraid of it. You have such a wonderful support system of friends
and family around you. Don't be afraid of the unknown. Embrace it, especially
when it's scary.

LOVE YOURSELF.
Wake up every day, and love yourself. Everything about you is perfectly you. Start really loving yourself now because if you wait, it makes it harder for me to do it later in life.

And give so many kisses to Dad, Mom, Lola Terry, and Grandma Didi. Give them hugs–especially Dad. Ask him questions, give him hugs for me, and tell him I love you. No reason why I'm honing in on Dad, just you know...time, it's been a long time.

Mara, you are one of the strongest people I know, and I've seen you go through some really high and really low moments in life, and guess what? We're still here, taking life one gay step at a time.

Listen to yourself, keep slaying, and I love you.

Love always,
Mara

Keep Playing - TR Deanon

Dear Nini,

How do you like being six years old? I bet you just finished playing outside with your cousins and your Kuya around the university where Dad taught. Did you play hide and seek around that building where there were so many nooks to hide in, and where people kept telling you to be quiet? (That was the library, by the way.) And every time you found a corner, you always hoped it would be the one that kept you hidden, but your heart seemed to scream THUMP-THUMP ready to give you away. Oh, such joy!

Did you slide down that hill on a huge coconut leaf sheath? You, your cousins, and your brother would collect at least six of these palapa ng niyog and run up the big mound only to go back down. I can just hear your squeals from when you and your Kuya ended up rolling down without the sheath because it is easier than sliding down in pairs.

I love that you love being outdoors. You saw the world as your playground, as it should be. You felt free outside, like you could roam all day and feed your curiosity with no one telling you what to do, and without you getting in any trouble. It was your chance to explore all that is around you, which led to you being curious about your body. You thought exploring your body would be just as joyful. Sometimes you just did it without any guidance. Wherever, whenever. Remember when you would just start playing with yourself while your whole family was watching a Sharon Cuneta movie because you didn't know any better? Mama would get so angry. She'd grab your hand and slap it. "We don't do that!" she would yell at you in front of everyone.

You didn't understand, and so you asked a lot of questions. What you were doing felt good; how could that be so bad? If you couldn't do it around people, why couldn't you do it by yourself either? But even if you lived with your grandmother, cousins, uncle, and aunt, no one gave you an answer. Instead, you always felt watched and confined.

So you started hiding. You would hold your breath hoping you won't get caught doing something that made your body feel good. But then again, Mama always found you. When you would go missing, she knew that you would be playing with yourself. She really did take the feel-good thrill out of hide and seek. Or maybe you were just really bad at hiding.

You hid this part of you because you thought you were a bad person based on how your mom reacted. Nobody was talking about it so you must have been the only one who was doing this bad thing, and it made you feel even worse. This is what we call shame, and unfortunately, this shows up because of how other people react to what we say, do, or are. But you're not "bad". You were curious, and you wanted to embrace your body.

To start getting rid of the shame, let me answer the questions you've kept to yourself.

Why is it that when we rub certain parts this way, it feels good?

The part that you're rubbing is actually called a clitoris. That's the most sensitive part of your body. And when touched the right way, it can feel magical. For example, do you remember how every time you see your favorite dessert, palitaw, and the second you put it in your mouth, you just always release a noise, like it's the best thing in the world? It's kinda like that.

Why does my body look like this, but my cousins look different?

I know you're asking this question because you, your brother, and your cousins would always bathe at the same time and you noticed that they all had the same parts that you didn't have. It is because some people have a vulva and some people have a penis, and these are called genitals. Others may even have both genitals or none. Every body is different and that's completely okay. We love what makes us unique.

Why does Mama make me feel bad about it?

I think Mama never had a conversation with Lola about this, so she didn't know how to discuss it herself. And maybe she thought that if you weren't allowed to touch your own body, you'd learn not to let anyone else touch it. Maybe that is her way of protecting you, and for her, that was the best thing she could do as your mom at that time.

Why would I stop when it feels good?

You shouldn't. When you're alone, do it as much as you'd like. There is nothing wrong with that. But it is a really intimate moment so you don't want to do it in front of everyone or with just anybody. We'll talk more later when it comes to other people joining in.

Why is it that it's always a boy and a girl who are together?

Because everyone around you is Catholic, and your family assumes that since you have a vulva, you're a girl and that you like boys. Based on what they've gathered from the church, that is how it's supposed to be. If not, you are a sinner and you will go to Hell. And whew, that was something you really held on to for a while.

Now, it's my turn to ask a question: Can I tell you something?

You actually don't like boys. Nini, you don't even really identify as a girl.

I'm sure you're confused and that's okay. Keep asking questions. You'll learn more as you get older. Just know that I'm so proud of you for continuing to explore your body even after hundreds of times Mama told you not to. At six years old, you were already holding on to the feeling of freedom, breaking away from being confined, and creating your own pathway for your future self.

Keep playing, okay?

 I love you.

TR (This is what you go by now, btw.)

LESSON SEVEN

MEDIA HAS THE POWER TO CHANGE LIVES.

One of my favorite television shows of all time was Joss Whedon's *Buffy the Vampire Slayer*, which ran for 7 seasons from 1997 to 2003. I can hear the first four notes of the theme song as I write this. The show ended just over 20 years ago, but the storylines and the characters still resonate with me today. I wanted to be one of the *Scoobies* and I may have even had a little crush on Sarah Michelle Gellar. I most definitely had a crush on actor, Wentworth Miller, who appeared in season 2, episode 20, "Go Fish."

I've rewatched the series multiple times over in my lifetime and it is still a hit with me. When the show originally aired on television, I would video record each episode on my VCR to (re)watch later. When DVD box sets of TV shows became a thing in the 2000s, my family spent more than $400 to purchase all seasons of the show. I realize that the price tag is incredibly hefty for DVDs, but I'm not even mad about it. Worth it. I loved reliving precious moments from the show. The DVDs still live somewhere in my parents' living room, by the way. When streaming content became a norm, I watched some of my favorite episodes online whenever I felt in the mood for nostalgia.

Buffy was one of the first shows I saw on television that challenged gender norms by placing a young girl, the title character, in the role of the superhero. This series showcased demons, ghouls, as well as supernatural and magical phenomena, which were access points to talk about taboo issues facing society and young people; it had multiple lesbian and queer-coded characters! It also cleverly showcased how "evil" characters were not always so evil and how "good" characters were not always so good. Spike was introduced to us as an evil vampire who overcame the odds to reclaim his soul and he proved to be one of the show's most celebrated heroes. Willow was a lesbian witch who was introduced as one of the goofy sidekicks, but almost ended the world when she became evil after letting her addiction to magic consume her life.

Perhaps this is an unpopular opinion, but the Willow and Tara love story will forever be greater than the Buffy and Angel dynamic. The queer romance we witnessed in the characters, Willow and Tara, was the duo that was meant to be, despite their unfortunate end. Buffy and Angel, the primary love story of the first few seasons, should have never been. I digress. The point is, this show changed my life and was one of the few opportunities I had when I was a child to think deeply about queer relationships, and whether having relationships as an openly queer person was even an option for me. *Buffy the Vampire Slayer* altered my perceptions of how life could be lived and it challenged how I thought about social expectations, social constructs, and people who were unlike myself.

·♥·♥·♥·♥·♥·

The previous chapter discussed the proverbial boxes we live in and encouraged us to step outside of those boxes. This chapter is about how mass media can be used to envision the world outside of our box. Media is a powerful entity whose job is to communicate broadly to audiences all over the planet. The messages carried through television, film, music, printed materials, radio, and all the rest are held closely by those who consume it. They show us the different ways in which we can view ourselves and each other.

Great storytellers can influence the masses, for better or for worse. Media can surely reinforce the constraints of the boxes we are told to live in. However, the most helpful use of media is to encourage us to imagine. Whether the stories told through media are based on fact or fiction, they allow us to imagine a life beyond our current circumstances or a world we can aspire to create. They can expose us to alternative lifestyles. Stories and images reflected in the media can challenge our perceptions as well as permit us to envision ourselves in a world beyond the box we've been told to stay in.

Exposure to new and different experiences as well as people can help us become more empathetic to diverse communities. Exposure provides opportunities to humanize unfamiliar groups of people. Exposure to the media allows us to get comfortable with new and different ideas that might not be observable in our daily surroundings.

If we had the awareness as younger queer Filipino Americans that the media had this level of power, I think we would be far more critical and selective of the media we consume. We would certainly take with a grain of salt, all of the images that reinforced stereotypes and fostered any negative self-perceptions. Lastly, if we knew the media could influence to push social movements forward, I believe we might have even demanded that content reflect our identities; and even leveraged media to a higher extent to showcase who we are and what we believe in. If we haven't already started doing these things, there's no day like today.

·♥·♥·♥·♥·♥·

In this chapter, the featured letters call attention to the stories and media that shaped the writers' lives and their perceptions of the world. As a Millennial, I was pleasantly surprised to see contributing writers mention TV shows, films, music, actors, and characters that were not only familiar, but prompted every nostalgic bone in my body to tingle. Some letters discussed how movies encouraged them to explore their own gender, sexuality, and ethnic identity. Some letters discussed how it was odd that characters from their favorite stories and shows were marketed to children according to gender. Other letters used their favorite media as a means to analyze their ambitions as well as relationships with friends and family.

CINDERELLA - JENSEN REYES

Dearest *bunso*,

I know you're not used to being called that, but I felt I had to grab your attention somehow. As I am writing this, the date is October 24, 2023. You are currently living in a 1-bedroom apartment in New York City and working at a bakery, spending your mornings baking croissants and making coffee and talking to people, while your nights are spent singing and making music. You live with your partner of 3 and a half years, another queer Asian American from Southern California, who got a job as a graphic designer in the city. So the both of you made a move 3,000 miles away from our families and everything that we've come to know. I know you feel a little different compared to your brothers or perhaps the kids at school, and I'm here to help you understand that a little better.

So last night we watched Cinderella. *Your* Cinderella, not the original animated version with the blonde princess, but the TV version with the pretty princess with the braids, who had a voice like silk, and a most fabulous fairy godmother, and a prince who looks like someone who could be one of your cousins at a family fiesta. I think you're maybe somehow still too young to understand the importance that that has, despite growing up in a majority-Latinx neighborhood in the majority-white area of southern Orange County. Soon, you will learn that you will be treated differently by some people because of the color of your skin, because of the shape your eyes make when you're at your happiest, and because of your last name. Or perhaps because of the way your hips move when you walk, or the way you prefer playing pattycake with the girls as opposed to playing fútbol with the boys. It is unfair, and I know you may still be oblivious to that, given that a lot of your friends and neighbors have similar complexions and similar names to yours. But soon you will journey into a much larger world and begin to experience so many things; so many things that will confuse you, yes, but also many things that will bring you clarity. Things that will ring true to the little child sitting cross-legged on the musty blue carpet of the living room in our shoebox condo on the "wrong side of town," eyes beaming at a prince and princess who look a little more like the people in your life.

Prince Christopher is played by Paolo Montalban in the 1997 adaptation of Rodgers and Hammerstein's Cinderella. Tall, charismatic, handsome, Filipino American, and a famous actor and singer; he's everything you wanted to be. There'll be moments while you're watching this movie wondering if you'll ever grow up to be like him, and in many ways, you will be, but as *I* grow older, I realize something about you, *bunso*. And that is for as many times as you have watched this movie, as many times as you have wondered if you'll ever be like him, and as many times as you have wondered if you end up falling in love with someone like him, you also don't fully see yourself in him, and that confuses you.

That confuses you because, for all intents and purposes, he is the representation that you so craved as a child. He is a young Filipino American man playing the lead role, singing songs, being emotionally available and vulnerable, and yearning for love. That confuses you because there's a small part of you that always saw yourself more as Cinderella:

A sensitive, romantic, imaginative young girl who spends her days playing make-believe and singing and daydreaming in the kitchen. As the youngest in her family, sometimes she feels misunderstood, or maybe like she isn't being heard. *Bunso*, I want you to know that I understand you, and I hear you.

Haven't you noticed how I haven't called you *sangko* or little boy, or anything else that would specifically reference your gender? That's because you've grown to live a life outside of the gender binary, which is just another way of saying you don't really consider yourself to be completely a "boy" or completely a "girl" for that matter. Nonbinary.

It's not impossible to see yourself as Cinderella and see yourself as the Prince. In fact, you can do that in any and every combination that exists (or hasn't even come to exist yet)! Don't you know that just because the world around you seems to be divided into "boy" things and "girl" things, that doesn't mean that *you* have to abide by those rules?

> *Don't you know that impossible things are happening every day?*
> *And if impossible things are happening every day, then why*
> *shouldn't you have impossible hopes and dreams?*

The following is a list of words I use in my current day to describe myself. I know this is a lot, and you're still, like, 4 years old or something, so I wouldn't worry myself too much with this, but consider it a self-fulfilling prophecy. You're bisexual. You're nonbinary. You're Filipinx, true, but you're also mixed with Teduray, Chinese, German, Spanish, as well as Scottish ancestry, and this becomes more apparent as you get older. I know these are just a bunch of words and they don't really completely fit you; sort of like how the glass slipper didn't completely fit the evil stepmother at the end of the movie. Because these words are not you, *you* are you.

You're Jensen. For as long as you dream and yearn that you'll find that special someone (and you will), you'll also learn that *you* are your own special someone. The relationship that you foster with yourself will be the longest relationship of your life. Other people may come and go. Even friends and family will go when the time comes. And I know that sounds scary, but at the end of the day, you will be with yourself for your entire life. It is of the utmost importance that you understand that *I* love you, okay? You love you, that's the most important thing that matters, okay? Finding your "one true love" isn't so important when you learn that you are capable of fostering love all around you and that it isn't found in just a single person.

I want you to continue loving the color pink, I want you to continue spending time with Mom in the kitchen, to keep watching Cinderella even when the other boys tease you for it. And I want you to continue spreading your love and allowing love into your life.

> *Don't you see? You're gonna spend your entire life yearning for a love like Prince Christopher and Cinderella. You're gonna keep imagining yourself as the Prince, or as Cinderella, but ultimately it doesn't matter because they will still embrace each other at the end of the movie, right?*

They are you. You are the prince *and* the princess. When they're embracing, that's you embracing all of yourself. And before you say "How can I be both, how can I embrace myself?"

Don't you know that impossible things are happening every day?

With all my love,
Jensen Reyes

Love Letter to a Late Bloomer - Paul Jochico

Dear PJ,

It's okay to take the long road to find yourself.

It's okay that you like to play with both Ninja Turtles action figures and Sailor Moon dolls. That's so odd, right? Why would toys marketed to boys be called "action figures" and femme-marketed toys be called "dolls." You intuitively knew better from the beginning and created a multiverse with whom they all could co-exist in an epic battle between good and evil. And all before multiverse epics became a trend! GO YOU!

In this multiverse, you can be more expansive than the gender norms placed on you by Filipino-American culture. You don't have to be the strong silent type or the macho guy to be accepted. You were already queer-ing the system as a child by embracing your feelings and vulnerability. This is one of your superpowers, and it creates a ripple effect to encourage other men in your life to be vulnerable and allow for intergenerational healing.

You've always had a brilliant mind. An expansive creativity that held the multitudes of what the world could be. Of who you longed to be. Before speaking them out loud, you play out the movie with every line and every alternative ending in your mind, and for a long time, you keep that film tucked away in the far-right corner of your inner world.

You say to yourself, *"I'm not allowed to have these kinds of dreams."*

"I'm not allowed to have these kinds of feelings."

"I've never seen anyone who looked like me live that life, be the main character, let alone have a happy ending."

Speaking of happy endings, it's okay that you feel something for both Meg and Hercules and then later have that same feeling for Lana Lang and Clark Kent. They will awaken a desire that is both exciting and terrifying at the same time.

You, as the only child of strict Catholic immigrant parents, have a long list of rules to live by and constantly walk a fine line.

"No English in the house because you will lose touch with it, with all the English you speak in school." Let's be honest though, we know it's really because they

want a code language they can use to scold you in public. At least back then...
You'll appreciate being multilingual many years later.

"No talking back to your parents because they are always right." You'll later
realize that they were kids themselves when they had you, and they were and
are figuring it out along the way just like the rest of us. They just committed to
their character a little more.

For a long time, you choose the path of least resistance. You play the role of the
perfect son. The sole container of your parents' hopes and dreams. You get really
good at being a shapeshifter and walking that fine line with ease. This is one of
your other superpowers!

You are an undercover spy like Jennifer Garner in *Alias*. Able to adapt to any
environment and situation. Able to thrive wherever you were planted. But you
become a mirror of what people want to see. Of what people want you to be.
Your parents. Your friends. Society.

One day you'll realize that keeping that seed buried deep within will only hurt
you. You can't make everyone happy, and you can't act through life in a script
that someone else wrote.

So one day in the future, you'll have that a-ha moment, and you'll start living
your authentic life. You'll start writing your story, and you'll let others see into
that beautiful creative mind of yours.

With an open heart that has a lot of love to give, you will bloom. You'll become
a different kind of mirror.

You don't know the word yet, but you'll understand the deep meaning of the
word *kapwa*: To see yourself in the other.

That mirror will help you realize how beautiful you are and how interconnected
you are to other people, the land, and beyond. You'll realize that love is the
energy that powers this connection and that your love is pure and unconditional
regardless of who you share it with.

I know that it's scary to open your heart to love right now. It'll take three decades
for you to embrace the fullness of who you are, so trust me I know...

I'm traveling through non-linear time to give you a big hug. I'm lifting you on my shoulders to show you that life is bigger and more expansive than the stories of what your parents, church, and mainstream society tell you about who you should be.

But it's also okay if it takes time to take a risk and let your heart crack open so that the seed that was always there can bloom. I love you for opening up your heart and giving love a chance again and again.

Knowing your true self and returning home to yourself is the journey of a lifetime.

And for what it's worth, I know you are afraid to bloom into your fullest expression in front of your parents, but these are the same parents who got you those Ninja Turtles "action figures" and Sailor Moon "dolls." They even got you a pink Little Mermaid suitcase to keep those toys in. I think deep down, they knew the truth and loved all of you in the best way they knew how.

In fact, one day, they'll tell you separately that you're the best thing that's happened in their life, and eventually, you'll realize they mean it.

Thank you for being brave.

Thank you for being curious.

Thank you for choosing love and taking the long way home to yourself.

Thank you for realizing that you were meant to bloom, doing so on your terms, and reminding those around you to bloom as well.

Mahal Kita,
PJ

You Are Not the Filipino Rachel Berry - Brandon English

Hey Senior Year High School Brandon,

I get that right now you're all about two big things: getting back with your ex and getting a lead role in The Wiz. But listen up, even if those things don't happen, the world won't crumble. Good news: You'll score a lead in The Wiz. Bad news: Your ex-boyfriend wants nothing to do with you and a bunch of people will turn on you. Yeah, you're gonna feel down and fed up for a bit, but you'll find out who your real friends are, and you'll pour your heart and soul into your art.

I know that you love Glee and want to be Rachel Berry or whateva', but please choose your role models wisely. The arts should be fun, so stop taking yourself so seriously. I know this is coming from a place of wanting to prove your *Toxic Titas* wrong about not being able to make it as a Filipino actor in the industry, but you need to do your art for yourself. It's okay to work hard and be ambitious, but stop being so hard on *yourself*. Perfection isn't real, and neither is the character Rachel Berry. Your worth isn't about what you achieve. Yes, you're aiming high and wanting to reach the stars, but honestly, slip-ups and setbacks won't make people think less of you. You're human, boo; so go easy on yourself.

I'm sorry that you're hiding your real self at home, worried your parents won't love you for being gay. I'm sorry you're stuck holding heartache while hiding it from them. And I'm sorry that you feel so lonely during this time of your life. This is all such a terrible burden, but don't shut people out, okay? The more you hide yourself from others, the less people will actually know you. I want to challenge you to be yourself, even when it's difficult. Give people a chance to love you because you are so lovable.

I just want to say, it'll all work out and your future is blessed because you've really come into your own and you're still growing. Everything that you once hated about yourself will be what you celebrate the most. Yes, you'll still have diva tendencies, but you're going to help so many people build their confidence and careers. Yes, you'll still work your ass off, but you will be doing it for yourself and not to prove anything to others. And yes, your ex-boyfriend still will never get back with you, but you've now found the love of your life.

You're actually killing it! I love you so much.

Present Day Brandon English

PERSONAL MYTHOLOGY - NICHOLAS PILAPIL

Dear 10-year-old Nicholas,

Congrats on a decade of life, and welcome to double digits! Relish in this milestone coming of age because the joy of getting older won't last forever. Sweet 16 will be fun, but don't be a brat when your parents buy you a used car for your birthday. It's gauche—plus, they'll buy you a brand new one when you start college. In your twenties, your post-college adult friends will rightfully read you down for unknowingly being a privileged brat. My advice: go and work on that now...

Adulting at 18 will feel like just another year because you'll already have been a smoker for five years, and you find no pleasure in buying Quick-Picks and playing the lottery. That said: don't curiously smoke that Pall Mall with Jazmin in the schoolyard between your house and the K-Mart. Smoking causes wrinkles—also cancer. Then 21. Unfortunately, this will be the last time it will feel fun to gain a number in age. Your drink of choice is a crisp and chill chardonnay. But you're not gay enough to sip white wine at a bar, so you drink gin and tonics in public. Also, there's no shame in drinking a mimosa outside of daytime hours.

But today you are 10. This is the age you start to cuss, discover that behind the kaleidoscopic static of channel 87 is porn, and become obsessed with Greek mythology and the TV show *Charmed*. On the flip side, this is also the age when the feeling of shame will slither into your life, sink its teeth into you, and the poison of it will slowly seep into everything you do. Its toxicity is something you will spend years trying to detox. Sorry, Kiddo, real life sucks, and sadly soon, you'll begin to understand why.

But don't freak out. This letter isn't like when you discovered you were a Cancer from the vending machine fortune teller at Universal Studio Walk. Where in exchange for a dollar, it shot out a piece of paper with your zodiac sign typed in bold Helvetica. The word "Cancer" fills you up with fear, reading like a diagnosis and a prophetic death sentence rather than a confirmation of your dramatic—yet loving—personality traits. Think of this letter as a premonition like Phoebe has in *Charmed*—a cute forewarning of what's to come. Believe it or not, this message is about love.

Faggot, *bakla*, girl, cholesterol—are slurs being slung at you right now from every direction. Boys at school taunt you. Miss Brownie calls a parent-teacher conference because she's concerned your only friends are girls. And your family, stuck in their Filipino ways, have concern and disdain for your femineity—and the Leonardo DiCaprio poster you pinned onto your wall. However, don't be reined in by the hate, because the names they call you aren't fact. You don't have high cholesterol and never will—you're vegan now. Although, you will suck a dick in college. And eventually, you write a critically-acclaimed play about butt sex and being Filipino American. Nicholas, you contain multitudes.

By the way, channel 87 is called The Spice Channel (Spice as in hot and sexy, not as in Spice Girls). You become obsessed with the secret of it. You spend late nights in the darkness of your room, combing through the static, like a needle in a haystack, for a glimpse of male nudity. The ratio between an unveiling of boob over a hard cock is 70:30. Nevertheless, your fervor for a glimmer of the male form answers what those Lolos have questioned, "Are you *bakla*?"

Your burgeoning desire terrorizes you, forcing you to believe that what you want is sinful. Your natural disposition doesn't align with the expectations of being an only child, an only son, the eldest grandchild, first generation, Catholic, and Filipino. It drives you mad, causes you to feel unworthy of the life you're given, and becomes the foundation of the barricade you inevitably construct around yourself to hide your truth from seeing the light. This is the shame I told you about, and the poison is that you will not only shield yourself from your family but will also shield yourself from even you.

You cast blame on everyone around you for the ways you feel small. And, yes, some people are to blame, but take some responsibility, too, because it's your fault for not being brave enough to be yourself. Be brave. Don't sulk in the darkness of others' perception of you for too long. You cannot control how the world will bend to you. You can only control how you bend to the world. Don't bend.

About right now, you're probably camped out in the library, lost in a book about Greek mythology. But why it gotta be Greek? Did you know that Filipinos have their own mythology, too? Our very own slew of deities, creatures, and stories. Here's a tale I want to share...This story is about two gods falling in love: Sidapa, the God of Death, and a moon God named Libulan. Sidapa lives on the highest mountain, so high that he could see the seven moons dancing across the sky from his domain. Spellbound by the beauty of the moons, Sidapa hails the birds and mermaids to sing his praises to them. In turn, the flowers send sweet perfumes to the heavens, and the fireflies shine bright to illuminate a path for the moons to find their way to him. The lithe Libulan answers Sidapa's loving cry and descends from the sky, and Sidapa rains Libulan with gifts and love. Then, in a rage of jealousy, the Sea God Bakunawa rises from the waters to devour the moons. But Sidapa, driven by his passion, saves Libulan from Bakunawa's wrath. To this day, Sidapa and Libulan live on that same mountain happily ever after as *husbands*. This myth has uplifted Libulan as a symbol for queer Filipinos, and today he is known as the Patron God of Homosexuality.

I tell you this because soon, the rippling insecurities you have about your identities will lead you to become estranged from your Filipinoness. You will blame history and culture as the reasons you don't feel accepted. You will be convinced that your uniqueness leaves no place for you to claim your heritage. But always remember the story of Sidapa and Libulan. Filipinos sometimes won't understand you, and your family will spew ignorance. But your queerness can live hand in hand with your Filipinoness. It's proven in the mythology of your people, and myths are a reflection of the people who believe in them. You are valid—and immortalized by the Gods. Be like the moon and illuminate the dark.

As an adult, you continue to be an avid reader and evolve into a writer as well. You find solace in all forms of storytelling. So, when you are feeling down and out, find yourself again in stories. Recount the myths that fascinate you, rewatch the TV that thrills you, and dive back into the books that capture your heart. In them, you will find inspiration and strength to come back into your own. Decades from now, you will still even watch *Charmed*—and be just as obsessed with it. You find comfort in rewatching episodes of the unstoppable Halliwell sisters using The Power of Three to protect the innocent and save the world. Even in a campy show like this, there's a lesson to take. And it's this: tap into your Power of Three.

With this letter, I offer you the power of **Prophecy**. Prophecy is the power to have divine realization. You will find that in your writing and the stories you tell. With this glimpse into the future, I gift you the power of **Perseverance**. Perseverance is having the ability to show up even though you know the struggles ahead. It is meeting strength with grace. Remember to stay strong and be kind to yourself. Lastly, with that reminder of self-love, I grant you the power of **Presence**. You can't change the past, but you can create a future by tuning into the present. Happiness doesn't flourish by dwelling on what's missing in your life. Happiness thrives when you can see the gifts of what's already in front of you. Happy Birthday!

Okay, bye.
Nicholas

FOR THE BOTH OF US - JONNY ALIGA

Dear Jonny,

You went to Beyoncé's concert in your hometown which happened to be on her birthday. I have never felt more alive for the first time in a long time. I know you're hiding every trace of liking Beyoncé because you're "supposed to be a man" and a "man" can't idolize a female artist. There's gonna be a song on her future album called "Church Girl" and one of the lyrics goes "Nobody can't judge me, but me. I was born free...". If there's any advice I would give you, it would be that; who cares if liking Beyoncé doesn't follow your family's perception of what a man is? Music is supposed to soothe the soul and not be a prerequisite to being a man.

The reason I share this with you is because the concept of masculinity will forever affect your life, whether you realize it or not. It will manifest itself in the way you form friendships and relationships. You don't see it now, but all the times you tried to help Dad at one of his plumbing jobs, he'd tell mom, *"Hindi siya totoong lalaki"* (He's not a real man); or when mom would walk in on you watching *Friends*, she'd say, *"Para lang yan sa mga babae"* (That's only for girls). Those experiences even still to this day sting and you will continue to have these experiences. Most recently, one of your cousins remarked how she'd never seen you dress "manly" before...when all you were wearing was a gray long-sleeve and black jogging pants...

Moments like those are so frustrating. However, they're a product of their environment and generation as much as you are of yours. Also, their perception of what being a man is a result of the male figures they had in their lives. I know you did not have any prominent male figures in your life besides dad; and I know there will be times when you will wish you grew up in a household where all of your cousins were male instead of female; or times you will wish your second mom, *Ate Dit Dit*, was a male instead. This will make you wonder how your life would've played out under those circumstances. Would Mom and Dad's desire for their son to be a "real man" be satisfied? Would you have become a baby daddy by now? Would you have multiple girls on your phone? Would you still be a homosexual? There are so many ways your life could've played out, but Jonny, I think the one you are about to live and experience is what is meant to be...for both of us.

With Love,
Jonathan

Embrace and Love Every Part of You - Jeff Deguia

Dear baby gay Jeff,

It's the summer of 2009 and you finally are coming to terms with who you are. You've joined the mysterious world of *Downelink*, an early social media site that was mainly for queer folks of color which was popular on the West Coast. It was an entirely new world for us, we saw other young gay people that looked like us. They were Asian, most notably Filipino. We have never felt so seen, especially since back in Chicago, gay and out Asians seemed like a rare species. These guys were kind of like me but were so much cooler. They wore fitted caps, had lip rings, and gauges - it was giving late 2000s Swag-a-Pino, for sure.

You are 19, and we're finally being honest with ourselves. Finally being proud of this part of you. Like many newly gay men at the time, you said you were bisexual (this is not bi-erasure though because bisexual people definitely do exist.) You have this heir about you though that you only like masculine guys. You have repeatedly typed out this extremely cringe-worthy and incredibly problematic phrase multiple times, "If I wanted to date someone feminine, I would just date a girl." To this day, I still hate that this was where our head was at. It took us until our mid-20s to really think about how fucked up and problematic this was.

In the future, there will be more conversations around "preferences;" and the "no fats, no femmes, no Asians" conversation has become mainstream on social media. We soon start to realize that exclusion within the community is so fucked up. We learn and fully understand that everyone in the community is important, that we all bring something different, and that creating division or some type of social hierarchy is gross. You begin to embrace the femme boys in your life and start to open up to more feminine things. You give props where it was deserved whether it was makeup, fashion, witty reads, drag, and so forth.

And importantly, you realize one major reason why we had this early disdain for feminine things. As a closeted youth in our teens and early college years, we didn't like the stereotypes; and we didn't like what non-queer folks associated with being gay, because their vision of it was so skewed. In mainstream media at the time, it was the feminine queer characters who got teased and beaten up. They weren't written with depth and they were rarely heroes of their own stories. Even in Filipino culture, though there is public love for gay celebrities on shows, within the Filipino community it wasn't welcomed especially in our family. You would catch lots of Tagalog and Ilocano conversations where the family would speak poorly of the LGBTQ+ community. Early on, after we came out, you desperately wanted to be loved by our parents. So that meant working against what a "typical" gay guy was like and forcing myself to play more into the masculine parts of me while downplaying the feminine things I liked.

From 2018 to 2020, things started to really change. We start to lean in on the more feminine parts of ourselves. It wasn't anything celebratory, we weren't throwing ourselves a parade, but in all the small ways, we allowed ourselves to live and explore. We start to see the fun clips of Drag Race; we start to openly and respectfully compliment women and femmes on their nails or their engagement rings; and we would get introduced to the ballroom scene. It started with *Pose* and then *Legendary*. You start to learn about the beautiful world created by Black transwomen in New York City. As you became a fan of both shows, you would spend hours watching clips from balls on YouTube and learning more about these talented individuals. You learn they were finding ways to express and be their true selves, without boundaries and with courage. This inspires us tremendously. For so long you hold back out of fear of how our family, friends, and world would see and perceive you, but you found some of the best inspiration in some truly special artists and creatives.

The main message to you, young baby Jeff, is to not hold back and to live out loud in any way that you please. I hope you find community and go after the hobbies and interests you want. You can discover a whole world of what it means to live proudly and loudly.

Take your time but don't let fear or anxiety hold you back. It's a long journey to be authentic and comfortable in your own skin and self because you're still doing this in your 30s. But don't worry, the journey is never over. Queer joy looks different in each of our chapters and we deserve to live our best lives for our elders and ancestors who could only dream of this freedom and reality. We live out loud for them and also for the younger ones after us.

Go out and find your queer joy.

With wisdom and guidance,
Jeff at 34 years old

Your Quiet - Blaine Valencia

Dear Blaine,

Out of the days that will pass you over in your colorful life, the one I write to you from sounds quieter than most. You achieved that. You arrived at quiet, but you might be more used to it than you realize.

I write from Los Angeles, where the only noise I'm picking up on at this predictably late hour is a gentle hum from the type of air conditioning unit that your family was never able to afford. It seems earlier generations had always been more reliant on sweat to cool their temperatures. The sounds here remind me of the sounds in your bedroom, with that one fan buzzing probably during an hour when you're the only one awake. I think of moments where sounds boomed—of 8:00 AM gossip, arguments on the phone over land, hoses quenching the thirst of a backyard garden, Brother blasting saxophone, Mom blasting ABBA, Dad blasting The Eagles, Grandpa blasting Ilocano folk tunes about butts. With time, all of that eventually rounds out to your quiet as you sit in the room with the door closed and the sun resting. The volume is down, but it's also that room where, in your reality, sound may have been the only thing quiet.

You may have made the walls loud when you asked to get them painted the brightest possible red. Maybe the color of your Grandpa's sardine cans somehow represented your flame and evergreen Scorpio intensity. Surrounded by red, you'd exist restless on your bed and inhale books, movies, shows, narratives, and tales of human triumph and despair and emotion and depth, all at a frequency I'm not sure I've ever matched since. You'd spend unusual time on random discussion forums and Tumblr, putting some of your earliest exercises in taste and artistry into practice. You'd perhaps curate and weave meaning into a visual and written galaxy that, in your eye, represented something beautiful.

The loudness, the volume of all that intake, proved this bright red setting as the birthplace of so many of your truths. No matter how ordinary it feels to scroll through webpages, no matter how many times you blast Kendrick or Gaga or Kanye on loop, know that these moments in your mind, with red walls as witness, built you a home in that house. And over time, know that you'll learn to pocket that quiet red, take it places so home for you grow into something boundless. That quiet, that red, is the place you became and the place you continue to become.

Today, the walls are still red, but the room is hardly yours. Today, the paint accompanies Dad as he knocks out between work shifts that have been oddly timed our whole lives. That room remains the darkest in the house. Before his bedtime, Dad now disrupts that darkness with a phone screen backlight, catching up with friendships through whom he taught you by example to cultivate. His method, and now yours too, has been to shrink thousands of miles of oceans and land masses with calls, video chats, and Christmas cards.

In your day, those red walls were your training grounds. They provided a setting for you to try out Mom's work ethic, and then later settle into your own. Red paint may have observed you and your own bright screens, with you and some imagination typing away, playing with big worlds and big words far too massive to contain in a thirteen-inch display. There, you'd be hyper-fixated on games like Pokémon, training to create a team with type match-ups that prepared you to handle what felt like anything. With your Tyranitar, Gengar, or Blissey in rotation, it never mattered how many times you lost, because what you created were fruits of your diligence and will that has never since faded.

Maybe you opted for Pokémon—or any other random bouts of rumination, overthinking, creativity, endless scrolling, or songs on loop—as avenues for safety when the grate of day-to-day life got harsh. In destinationless trains of thought, the walls may have witnessed you sitting still, revisiting in your mind instances where those around you may have asked or imposed or assumed or called you names or acted out of ignorance or cruelty that may have grated against your flesh with the metallic depth of a knife. Maybe each grate culminated into a gash. Maybe each gash showcased a raw open wound, scarred over.

And so you sought safety and created it yourself. With a red witness, you may have stepped away from a world of Hail Marys and Our Fathers and Creeds that may have shoved you entrapped in your not yet liberated queer flesh and being. It's there where you sat with your stomach twisting, processing and reprocessing, playing back over and over and over the zigzags of your glance in locker rooms and underwear aisles, the activities of your adolescent curiosity, or the kisses and hastened heartbeats. You'd try and brush all of it off when probed about any of this by others. But most times, you'd be left with yourself to devour this all internally.

And in that devour, you swallowed whole. And so you disentangled, and so you discovered acceptance and birthed your glow. In this quiet, you battled, won, and rehearsed holding space for multiple, seemingly contradictory truths to co-exist in deep calm.

Those red walls taught you to embrace divinity elsewhere. It called you to experience, if even for a moment, what it means for intimacy to expand universes. Your quiet instructed you to slow—to breathe gentle breath, and to grow with the same patience as the flora and fauna embracing the landscapes cozy with the horizons, then grow more, like the green pockets of creation Grandma nourished and watered. It's here where imagery passes through you with such vividness that you can hear the winds kiss as the waves break. It's in this sense of place where you've envisioned visions, felt toes sandy, stomachs full, with laughter as background melody, and sat safe and surrendered to the type of chatter and company and connection and community where souls pour into one another without limit.

Trust that you will inhabit journeys in your days to come. Your eyes will widen. Your store of stories will multiply and become richer. You will hear songs that register a resonance that you have yet to encounter. You will find people whose quiet rings the same tune as yours, people whose quiet cracks yours to no longer be something lonely, but infinite. Seeds you've already planted blossom into a magnificence that you will soon cherish and hold onto tightly.

Every single thing you did in that quiet red—every thought that passed, every pocket of creation, every quiet realization, every imagined escape, every labored effort, every bout of anger, every solitary teardrop, every scribbled word—all of it, created something I love. You'll learn to love it all, too.

Blaine

LESSON EIGHT

FINDING LOVE AND BEING LOVED IS A DAMN JOURNEY.

Dawson's Creek featured a cast of actors in their 20s playing teens on TV. (Yes, I watched *Dawson's Creek*.) Multiple storylines followed the adventures and love triangles of hopeless romantic high schoolers. One character at the end of season 3, Jack McPhee, played by Kerr Smith, made television history by sharing an on-screen kiss with another male actor, on a primetime TV show marketed to teens.

This was the season finale episode which aired in 2000; that moment was a big deal in pop culture history. While for me it was welcome to see two guys share a smooch on one of my favorite TV shows, there are still issues I grappled with when it came to this moment; when it came to this show in general. The storyline that followed Jack McPhee in *Dawson's Creek* reinforced that homophobia was alive and well. Jack was talked down to by a teacher who then proceeded to force him to stand up in class and read a private poem he wrote, which revealed his attraction to a male classmate. "FAG" was spray painted in large, red, capital letters across Jack's locker by homophobic peers. Jack was a brave character, but the message I took away from these moments was that it was not safe to be queer.

There was also a serialized TV drama called *Queer as Folk,* which ran in the U.S. from 2000 to 2005 on the Showtime Network. I remember as a 14 or 15-year-old, kid, being eager to sneak peeks at this show. Of course, I couldn't openly watch it without feeling like I was outing myself. To be honest, there were many problematic takes featured on this show, including the romanticization of a relationship between a 17-year-old high school student (*Justin Taylor* played by Randy Harrison) and a 29-year-old advertising executive (*Brian Kinney* played by Gale Harold). Regardless, *Queer as Folk* was meant to cater to gay men of the 2000s, yet somehow I still did not feel like I was adequately reflected in this program. The storylines centered on White gay men, their issues, and adventures. Still on this show, like on *Dawson's Creek*, there was a scene that seared into my brain. Brian races down a neighborhood street in his Jeep Wrangler to drop Justin off at school the morning after their hookup. The vehicle comes to a screeching halt right in the center of the frame to reveal the extent to which it had been vandalized. The word "FAGGOT" was spray painted in large letters across the outside of the front and rear passenger-side doors.

In both of these examples, the stigma of same-sex romantic relationships was highly prevalent. In both, the main characters were predominantly White and conventionally attractive. Sometimes it felt like White and conventionally attractive were different terms for the same thing. White faces and slim bodies set the standard of beauty during this era of television and film. I did not see very many Asian/Filipino personalities on the screen who could remind me that Filipinos were beautiful, desirable, and worthy of love. *Enter the 2000s versions of Paolo Montalban, Vanessa Minnillo, and Nicole Scherzinger from stage left to discredit my points.

·♥·♥·♥·♥·♥·

Ultimately, as a queer Filipino kid in the United States during the 90s and aughts, I did not feel worthy of love. In the previous chapter, we saw how media, for better or worse, can be a powerful tool to influence our perceptions of self and others. I do believe my idea of what love and romance were supposed to be was skewed based on the media I consumed and based on the expectations placed upon me by my friends and family. Because American culture predominantly set the stage for me to be presented with media and messaging touting the desirability of an unrequited romance and love with White men and women, I felt perpetually in a never-good-enough state of being.

When queer Filipinos make it to that point where they feel comfortable enough to start pursuing friendships or romantic relationships with other queer people, racialized standards of beauty make themselves well known. The letters featured in this chapter reflect the inner thoughts of individuals who have struggled with the experience of dating, romance, and relationship building. Some letters will discuss the racialization of romantic or sexual encounters with others. Some letters will tackle the inner struggles of accepting that they have romantic feelings for someone of the same gender. Other letters reflect upon the long journey it takes to find a romantic partner.

·♥·♥·♥·♥·♥·

Dating is hard. Relationships are hard. I think back to when I was a closeted teenager. I thought, "If I could just find the courage to date, my life would be better." I started dating girls. It was okay, but I still felt empty. I thought, "If I could just date guys, I would feel happy." There's immense liberation attached to finally being able to explore a same-sex relationship. However, I found myself feeling like I was dependent on another person to make me happy. I thought then, maybe I just hadn't found the right person. I thought maybe if I could just change myself into something others might desire, I could get someone to commit to me. If I were slim enough; strong enough; youthful enough; talented enough; smart enough; rich enough; maybe I'd feel worthy of love. I was never happy in that mindset of always looking for more. This is all backwards you see. You have to believe you are worthy of love before you go out and pursue relationships to add to your life. For queer Filipino Americans, it may feel like it takes ages to get to self-acceptance and self-love. But that's truly a prerequisite to healthy friendships and romantic partnerships.

You are complete and lovely as you are.

HANDLE WITH CARE - JEFF DEGUIA

Dear young, hopeless romantic Jeff,

I can't remember a time when you weren't firm in your romantic and emotional side. Even your middle school girlfriends were treated with deep affection. For the longest time, I know you've yearned to be loved and cared for in the way that you love others. You've wanted it so much that you've stayed in *situation-ships* that have lasted way too long because you hopefully and naively believed it was going to work out. What is even more painful was how long it took you to move on. I think having a big heart can sometimes be a double-edged sword. In one way, you have so much love to give, but on the other hand, all the love given with vulnerability and openness can lead to deep heartbreak.

You used to frustrate me a little bit, but I cradle you now. I hold you deep within and shield your sweet and sensitive heart. I remind you that your lack of relationships or unreturned romantic love isn't a reflection of you or your worth. You are extremely worthy of genuine and healthy love. You simply have chosen the wrong men to pursue. Essentially you were "blinded by love" and gave your heart to people who didn't deserve it. My main thought is that I wished you had moved on sooner from the past because so much of your mindset to take your time "to heal" was riddled with anxious thoughts. And that's only clear now since we've been to therapy. I will always admire your deep emotional capacity, but we hurt for so long because of what anxiety started to tell us and what we started to believe.

I don't want to say that I think you wasted your 20s because things happen for a reason. I'm happy to know that you've learned and haven't let these poor experiences affect you too much. I truly believe that it takes courage to continue to love bravely and openly, but now you know better about how and when to give love. I know dating again is a little scary, but I want you to remember what you know now. That's wisdom; that's growth. It might not be perfect and it will be hard work but it will all be worthwhile. I'm happy to see you bloom and mature in the way that you love. It's taken a lot of time, but we're here. You're in good hands now, your future version of yourself is taking care of himself and finally loving himself the way you have loved others. Young, hopeless romantic, Jeff. I'm so happy and relieved you made it through. But I'm even happier that you've grown up and matured and learned your lessons.

Love you always,
Jeff

WHEN YOU THINK YOU'RE HUNGRY - TIANO P.

dear tiano,

you wince as you open your eyes, realizing you fell asleep with the lights on

on your couch that feels as unforgiving as the shots you were throwing back at
the bar earlier that night. your phone says it's 3:21 am. the multiple texts from
different unsaved numbers, the clothes you wore out scattered around the room,
and the dull headache from the hangover that's settling in force you to shut your
eyes again.

you're about to let the sleep win when your stomach rumbles and feels an insa-
tiable need to be filled since you can't remember the last time you ate something
and

another text comes through from one of those mystery numbers: i could come
pick you up if you want.

you scroll back through the conversation to figure out who's offering to pull you
out from underneath this waterfall of shame that's pouring into your stomach's
emptiness because you somehow found yourself in this exact situation. again.

the only clue you find in this very, very short string of texts is a picture of a
faceless torso,

a faceless torso in front of his bathroom mirror, showing off a mesmerizing
tattoo on his forearm,

but you ignore the hypnotic tattoo, swipe out of the text, and close your eyes
again.

you clamp your eyes shut, hoping you can ignore the lights that are still on, the
headache that won't let you forget it's there, the tattoo that's lulling you into
the universe that exists within his mirror, and your very obvious nakedness that
has nowhere to hide because your clothes are waiting patiently around the room
for you to put them back on,

get in his car, send the same clothes off to their new home on the floor of his
apartment, fall into the puffy cloud that is his bed, feel him refill the hole inside
you that was overflowing with shame just an hour ago

until the shots from the bar come bubbling out of your mouth as a single word: stop.

the movement as he shows you his universe has you feeling untethered and unsettled, like you're floating through a world without rules

a world where the only thing you can do is

feel

feel the blinding lights that burn your eyes at 3:21 am, the rumbling in your stomach from the lack of food, the dullness of the headache thanks to your hangover, the neverending waterfall of shame, the fullness of his universe filling you

feel the glass of water he places in the palm of your hand, wraps your fingers around, and guides to your mouth

feel the coolness of the water as it flows down your throat and into the pit of your stomach, washing out the shame you felt as you sent him your address, the shame you felt as he took you through his universe, the shame you've accumulated from being in all those other guys' worlds.

suddenly, the hunger you felt lying on the rigidity of your couch in the depths of your hangover disappears.

listen.

sometimes, tiano, when you think you're hungry,

your body is telling you it's dehydrated. drink a glass of water.

with all the love and water,
tiano

IN AMERICA - JOBERT E. ABUEVA

Dear Jobert @ 18,

In America, you won't have your nuclear family of *tatay*, mommy, and siblings, though you'll come to love a different kind: Neil, Michael, Andy, Phil, and so many others, an extended clan of chosen ones, coming in and out of your nomadic and messy life. You'll relish these bonds. They'll be your safety net. And love you for who you are.

In America, folks will cringe when you joke that on July 4th, Philippine-American Friendship Day, all gay Filipinos find American boyfriends. You had heard it delivered by a *bakla* TV host while growing up in Manila and it stuck with you. Well, you repeat it over and over because it's what you truly desire.

In America, you'll fall for a married man on more than one occasion. As if to spit on the Catholic commandments of your upbringing. You'll argue we are helpless to love's pull no matter how rugged the terrain. You'll want to prove your detractors wrong. You'll find ways to make it work even though the ultimate lesson is that it never does.

In America, you may not necessarily have a partner to last a lifetime but a long-term relationship, a decent run of 19 years. You and Bruce will fall in love after business school, leave the city for a house in the country, adopt five dogs and a cat, start a business venture, and eventually drift apart. An amicable parting all things considered.

In America, you'll be single a few times over, even for an extended period well into your middle age. You'll be a third wheel in a community of couples. Pitied as you hang out at the bars. Ridiculed as you swipe the apps. Told "no Asians" and seldom with a "please." Even ghosted with nary a reason why.

In America, xenophobia and homophobia will rear their ugly head, both outright and subtle, ebbing and flowing though never fully dissipating. You'll witness the hatred in hearts, cry over senseless attacks, and make vigilance your default stance.

In America, loneliness will be a constant companion.

In America, you'll bring your authentic self to work. Colleagues will accept you for who you are, or at least be polite about it. You'll build a career working endless hours, hustling for promotions, traveling the world, and being well compensated. But you buy into the construct that an out immigrant must work thrice as hard to get ahead.

In America, you'll learn that you can't be friends with everyone.

In America, you'll write an op-ed on why you are finally leaving the Catholic Church. "The harsh, if not hostile, message towards the LGBTQ community is a tough pill to swallow for gay Catholics in America and the world over who have long had to walk the tightrope of our beliefs against a doctrine that continually turns a cold shoulder on this one aspect of who we are as holistic beings." Many will thank you, and just as many will say you're mistaken. All will pray for you.

In America, *pakikisama* will be your lifeline and weapon to assimilation and survival.

In America, hope springs eternal. You'll rise to the occasion and dust yourself off after every fall. You believe in second chances, and that being an optimist is what will save the day. Love might be lurking around the corner. So, you lean into its possibility. The sun's warmth on your face, the winds of life's travails on your back.

Welcome to America. What will truly be your land of the free?

With Love,
Jobert @ 60

Love Will Find You - Dr. Arnel Calvario Ripkens

Dear 35-Year-Old Arnel Calvario,

It took you 31 years to finally live your truth out loud and you are experiencing the ups and downs of gay dating.

Dating over the last few years started off exciting! You were finally out and proud and feeling like a kid in a West Hollywood men's candy store!

However, despite growing up so proud of your Filipino-American heritage, you are now encountering discouraging dating profiles with preferences stating "No fats, fems or Asians."

You will date lots of attractive guys, but many are going through life transitions, many "not ready to commit," some who will make you really doubt yourself, and several who just weren't the right fit for one reason or another.

I know you are starting to feel like the "last one" to find your person — the last of your siblings, the last of your college friends, the last of your old roommates, the last of your chosen gay family, the last of your high school friends, the last of your cousins...

Seeing all your loved ones getting married is evolving into seeing these couples now start families.

You are learning a lot of lessons while dating, but you also keep re-learning many of those same lessons.

Things really won't change until you start LIVING those lessons and lean into change.

Lucky for you, your bestie, Eric Jarvina, will guide you into finding your gay chosen family and all your closest, true family friends will stand with you through the test of time.

Our youngest brother, Eric Calvario, will marry his amazing husband Cliff and they will join our other amazing siblings in being our incredible family support system until Mom and Dad are ready.

After many years of looking, you will finally live your way into your mid-40s and turn your focus inwards.

With every person you dated, you learned something new about yourself in relationships and what you truly hoped for and deserve in a healthy relationship.

You will learn to dispel the critical voice inside your head that has always held you back.

You will learn how to value your time & energy more.

You will unlearn "people-pleasing" tendencies and learn that boundaries are amazing!

You will learn how to cultivate love, appreciation, & care within yourself and how to really dedicate time and energy to healing, cultivating self-worth, and self-love.

You will learn that all the parts of your identity together are what makes you EXTRAORDINARY in the world.

You will better balance serving others with making regular time for nourishing your mind, body, and soul.

Life experience, your resilient growth mindset, the support of loved ones, and weekly therapy will lead you to learn and live all these things.

Your family – blood and chosen – will not only continue to stand with you and lovingly support you, but they will champion you forward.

You will learn that the most important person to love first is YOURSELF.

Then at 45, just as the cliché rings true, love will find you "when you least expect it" and trust me...he will be worth the wait.

With Love,
50 Year-Old Dr. Arnel Calvario Ripkens

BOY-BAWANG NOSE - JONNY ALIGA

Dear Jonny,

Being Filipino is so hard when it comes to hooking up. You're gonna constantly come across guys who claim that they "love" Asians, but once you send a picture of yourself all of sudden, you get blocked immediately because of your tan complexion and your *Boy-Bawang*–looking nose. I guess what their bio meant to say is that they're looking for an Asian whose description is the opposite of that: Lighter skin and a perfectly concave nose. However, there have been others who think you're so cute and sexy, but also…not because of your face, but because of your "twink" or "boyish" body. And you'll take whatever you can get because you're so desperate for someone to want you. You want the intimacy your parents and your cousins have with their partners…you want it so bad even if it lasts an hour or hell, even 10 minutes. You just want to feel wanted.

I'm here to tell you it's not worth it and that they don't want you, they want your body. It's kinda hard to separate someone from their body, but they don't want you for you, they don't want all the good and the bad that comes with you. They just want you for the pleasure. They want that dopamine release when it's finished, so they can continue their life. But where does that leave you…where does that leave us? It leaves you in a place of loneliness, in moments where you're wishing and praying for someone to want and love you.

I know your sex life is the last thing you wanted to know about, but I just needed to let you know because it's one of the many things that contributes to the false narrative in your head that you aren't good enough and that the only thing you amount to being is a tanned twink. This is something I am currently working on, so I can't give you a proper send-off, but if I can say anything it is this – really love yourself Jonny, flaws and all. Love all your imperfections and that *Boy-Bawang* nose and know your worth so you can save your mental and emotional well-being for someone who will love and cherish you for you.

With Love,
Jonathan

THERE IS NO WORD FOR QUEER FEMME IN TAGALOG - DIANARA RIVERA

Dear 12-year-old Dianara,

You will hear the word *bakla* early in your lifetime. You will hear the word tomboy later too. Your mom will tell you not to cut your long, wavy hair up until high school, and both the boys and girls at school will ask you to touch it regularly and without abandon. You will let them because you want the attention, and you will not remember the times when you were little enough to live without long-term memory, coasting from military base to military base, the fluttery affections of little brown boys, and your mom's vicarious observing smiles.

You will see your mom's homeland one day. You will see it when you are 19, at a time in your life when the only way you know to be a person is to follow your feverish teenage amygdala. New to the metropolis and an Ivy League degree soon to be in your name, the Filipino boys will treat you like their own Miss Philippines, and you will have sweaty conversations across Manila's nightlife long past your most wishful preteen dreams.

It's okay that those dreams are attached at the hip with the haunt that you are doing it wrong. It's okay that your mom calls your first and deepest celebrity crush *bakla*, and that your dad clicks his tongue when your crush is seen making out with another man on national television. It's okay that the sweaty Filipino boys in the club are confused that all you want to do is talk to them all night, and that no matter how many shots they buy you, you lose interest in kissing them once the rush of skin on skin contact floats back up into the heat.

You will be mourning the loss of a situation-ship in which you thought you had feelings for a boy for the first time in your whole 19 years. You will be mourning the way you got so close to the dream you harbored ever since you read the word "scintillating" in Twilight during seventh grade reading period and thought, "Wow, boys must be so stunning for someone to use such a pretty word to describe them."

You will even think that maybe you loved him because you cried every night thinking that all the years wondering why you never had feelings for anyone were leading up to this one moment when even your reciprocal interest wasn't enough. You will even think that it is normal that when your friends ask you why you haven't had sex yet, all you know to say is that you've felt outside of your body for as long as you can remember, and all you know is you want the kind of love that your parents don't have, and that you don't know how to get. After years and years of never dating anyone, you will finally tell your mom that you were dating a boy and he broke your heart and she will ask if he is Filipino or American. You will say neither, he's an international student, and she will tell you "It's okay *anak*. You're so beautiful and *mestiza*, you have a nice body," just like she did when she was young. The boys will keep on coming because she was so popular in her province and you look just like her when she was young. It won't make you feel better, and you won't ever tell her about you dating again.

It's okay to feel bad that she didn't know how to make you feel better then, and still won't know how to later. She can't understand why your feelings don't make sense because you don't have the language to describe it and neither does she. You'll spend your life trying to find the language and it's never going to feel like enough. Sit in that not enoughness together and understand that it will be the way you bond for the rest of your life.

You won't ever get that close to your preteen dream again, and it's going to be the best thing to happen to you. The best thing that came from that summer in the Philippines? The beautiful and vulnerable Filipina community you meet and grow with. The first times you think you could like girls are drunken 4 a.m. conversations in the attic room you all share while you help your friends swipe on queer Manila Tinder. The first time you are in a deep relationship with someone who is queer and looks like you, is when your closest friend that summer already calls herself queer and you bond with her over conversations of love and community and what it means if love doesn't have to be attached to romance, and what it means if love doesn't have to be with men. Eight years later you will reconnect with a friend from that summer and she will come to your 27th birthday, and it will be like nothing has changed. She will say you're truly thriving now, that she didn't even remember celebrating your birthday in the Philippines because you were too shy to tell everybody back then. It will be the queerest birthday party you've had yet, and it'll make you laugh at all the times you tried your hardest not to let abandonment wash over you alone in your dorm room over spring breaks, or in your childhood home after school is out for the summer and you haven't talked to a friend in days.

You will take a writing class with author Chen Chen and he will say to find the sentimentality in both directions. The writing classes you will take in college will teach you that sentimentality is bad, that emotion is campy and unserious and god knows you want to be anything but that. The white girls in your classes will critique your half-finished depression-addled personal essays as messy, sentimental, almost there.

"Why don't you translate the word bakla? The phrase bahala na? Why couldn't you finish your essays in time for class" and "How come you're always writing about the same damn things?"

It will break your spirit. You will quit writing for years after you graduate, even though it was your dream for as long as you can remember. You will wonder what is wrong with you, if your words were ever really powerful to begin with. You will think– am I only a good writer when I'm depressed? Do I only know how to write about being gay? You will think the antidepressants you (finally) begin taking are robbing you of your creativity, of your longest, most cherished childhood dream. Those thoughts will never go away. But you will learn to let them scream, then pass. Like a freight train rushing by that you can't stop. Or, later in life, like a pesky rain-swollen cloud, so lazy it becomes annoying, but still harmless.

The sentimentality will be in both the failed boy crushes and the most blood-rush-to-your-head, mine all the words in the English language lesbian loves you will ever have. It will be in both the isolation of your childhood and the queer Filipino community you will later devote your every waking moment to build. It will be in the way your parents tell you to go to hell for going to therapy and the way the therapy will keep you in one place long enough for people to have a chance to show you love.

You'll figure out love. You'll figure out sex too. You'll be 21 the first time you are ever truly attracted (both physically and romantically) to somebody, and it won't be a man, and you'll be trying to describe what it felt like to others for the rest of your life. You'll be 22 when you think you fall in love again, and it will be a relief. You were thinking this whole queer thing was a mistake because you hadn't fallen for someone again since that first world-shattering time. You'll be 23 when you move to a new city as a freshly confident lesbian and you will gain the confidence you never thought you'd have when the pimply middle school boys were pretending to ask you out just to laugh with their friends about it later. You'll be 24 when you find serious, stable love. Love that lasts past the rain-swollen clouds and ever-present freight trains. You'll be 25 when you get a community organizing job with people that feel like family, and 26 when that job morphs into some artist-activist dream.

And throughout it all? Your mom will never understand you. She'll never understand your life, and she'll barely know the details of it. She will, however, know you've changed. She'll call you and say *"Ate*, you seem happier now. Are you happy with your job? You're not lonely anymore?" She'll know your partner even though she doesn't know you're dating, and she'll share your campiest, most complex dreams of love, success, and despite it all, family.

It's okay that all you know right now is this foreboding and a lot of feelings you have no words to name. It's okay if this seems like more than you can handle. All this has to happen, and it won't be easy.

You will know more than anyone just how strong you are, in not only your mind but your body, and no one will be able to take that breathless, wordless being away from you.

Love,
(a starting to heal) Dianara

Close Reading a Girl Crush — Alyssa B.V. Cahoy

Hi langga,

Even while you're still in that rural Louisiana town, part of the ~2% Asian population and diluting your brownness, know that you can remain true to yourself.

How is being true to ourselves possible? Flying proudly in the yard across from yours, a cloth emblem of white supremacy. Marked by a star-patterned X.

With your language. A powerful tool that colors the way we see the world and ourselves. I offer to you a liberatory practice, of what will germinate as a small, private act of minding your language, but will

unfurl into something
tall and manifest
that breathes life back into you.

Let's examine the phrase "girl crush" and the context you deliberately arrange to surround it
— the filler flowers used in a bouquet to draw attention from the awkward gaps between blooms.

You went to a public high school dance, and Mom told your friends not to let you get into any funny business. You didn't mind this because only boys are included in funny business. You still get to dance with the girls.

At most, they're "girl crushes." At least that's what you keep telling yourself and your girlfriends. (Careful, lest our inner monologue reinforce contrived truths.) Prefacing "crush" with "girl" as if it's a disclaimer that the Standard Crush^{TM} is one on a boy, and therefore a *girl* crush cannot be accepted as a legitimate crush. You are capitalizing on the plausible deniability of meaning the latter, that this "girl crush" is in fact a real one. You hope to God no one would think much of it.

Not only does that linguistic choice dim the vivid colors of your orientation, (*compulsory heterosexuality is in the room with us*), but it also fetishizes and undermines the validity of WLW, women who love women, and relationships. "Girl crush" implies dismissal. "Girl crush" language weaponizes your unfamiliarity with dialectical thinking.

I'm here as your now-*Ate* to tell you that it's okay to admit you have a crush.

She's your crush. You can have crushes on women.

Your attraction to other women will get harder to ignore when you move to the city. You hold your breath when Lucy walks past your seat in Spanish class.

The guy who asked you to his senior prom, Archer, was in varsity choir with Lucy and knew she admired him. He even found Lucy pretty cute. She is two years younger than him, a year younger than you. Archer, the unassuming guy that he is, just thought you were really easy to talk to and somehow immune to jealousy. Little did Archer know, there was a little love triangle you repressed, but nevertheless was present in your mind...

you : Lucy :: Lucy : Archer :: Archer: you.

You go through Lucy's Instagram intermittently, admiring the brightness in her demeanor, her unruly brown curls, and her charming smattering of facial freckles, wishing you could have her know what you really thought about her.

These days, you still follow Lucy on Instagram.

Whenever you feel at odds with yourself, pay close attention to your thoughts. How can you be more gentle? You don't have to pin yourself down with the stubborn language in your head. Let's give ourselves that kindness
— give yourself those flowers.

To borrow from Neferti Tadiar (a Filipina critical theorist whose works you will encounter in college), think of practicing mindful language as an "exercise in becoming," in which you can freely write your own story. Whether or not you are conscious of it, you *are* writing a story about yourself in your head. This "exercise in becoming" will be like coming home to yourself at last.

My hope is that this close *reading practice* will become a *living practice* for you. By paying closer attention to your thoughts, you can practice posturing yourself in the liberatory peace of self-acceptance.

And you can start by refraining from telling yourself you have a "girl crush."

Yours truly,
Ysa holding the figurative pen

LESSON NINE

You will experience loss and heartbreak

As a young boy, I used to write letters to my father's mother, my *Lola*, while she lived in the Philippines. We were pen pals. I loved keeping her up to date with my life in elementary school. For a time, she lived with my family in California as well. During those periods when she lived with my family, I used to love watching her brush her dentures. She held them in one hand and brushed them delicately with a toothbrush in the other. My father kept her comfortable. He always kept her warm water bottle close by; he kept Salonpas stocked; and made sure her walker was in working condition. At the time, Dad was a strong and sometimes scary man. I never saw him cry until his mother passed away. I was in middle school in the late 90s. For weeks and months after her death, I would find him shedding tears into a photo album. I was sad I would no longer have my precious pen pal.

I have fond memories of my *Lola* on my mother's side as well. She was so tiny and so quiet, but always visible. To me, she was a woman of few words. She made me smile once when she brought me and my cousins breakfast one morning. She placed a pink box on the kitchen counter and in her soft voice she said one single word, "Donut?" She hardly ever spoke, so it caught me off guard in a funny way. Everyone recognized her commitment to being present, especially for the kids. A tragic accident took her life in 2013; a careless act by a stranger. My aunts, uncles, and cousins on my mother's side lived all over the United States and the Philippines at the time of her passing. We all convened shortly after the accident to bury my *Lola* and to celebrate her life.

Both of my *Lolas* birthed many children, who birthed many children. To bear witness to grown adults crumbling into the helplessness of their grief is overwhelming. Fury. Melancholy. Hopelessness. Confusion. Regret. Denial. Imagine all of these emotions not only filling a room but also interacting with one another. Adults are expected to have a solid hold on their emotions, but grief can topple anyone. In my life, I have experienced the death or dying of others close to me and close to my family.

> *Classmates have passed away.*
> *Friends have passed away.*
> *Family members have passed away.*

Life is fleeting. I am guilty of thinking that the end is so far away. Sure, we have an idea of how much time we ought to have in this world based on the average age of death across the human population. The average life expectancy in the United States is anywhere between 70 and 80 years. Unfortunately, the average life expectancy in the United States has steadily declined over the last few years; in 2019, the life expectancy was about 79 years and it is currently about 76 years (Simmons-Duffin, 2023). Presuming most readers are adults, imagine yourself at age 10. Looking back at that first decade of life, doesn't it feel like that time went by in the blink of an eye? For me, that period of time flew by in what feels like a moment. Now consider you only get 7 or 8 of those *moments* (i.e. decades) of life. You'd be so lucky to get just a tiny bit more than that, but the sad reality is no one knows how much time any of us actually have left.

In a study of attitudes and customs surrounding death and dying amongst Filipino Americans, researchers found that while customs surrounding death were taken seriously, the preparation for and assistance with death and dying was not as prevalent (Braun & Nichols, 1997). Filipino Americans may participate in religious customs to honor the dead, such as 9 days of community prayer known as the *novena*, part of a Catholic ritual believed to aid the souls of the dead in their afterlife journey toward Heaven. However, less common are open conversations and efforts by Filipino Americans that would help them identify their end-of-life wishes and get other personal affairs in order.

The lack of conversation amongst Filipinos regarding the planning of death and dying may prevent us from having an accurate perception of how much time truly remains for ourselves, our communities, and our loved ones.

·♥·♥·♥·♥·♥·

As lovely as life can be, you cannot experience the good without experiencing the bad. This is especially true for folks who have historically been marginalized in this country. Queer people and people of color in America are constantly told they are not worthy; not good enough; not deserving of peace, and not destined for greatness.

May I remind you:

> *You are worthy.*
> *You are better than good enough.*
> *You do deserve peace.*
> *And you have been great; you are allowed to rest.*

While it's true that you cannot reach positive life milestones without overcoming the struggles that are associated with your queerness and your Filipino-ness, it is important to acknowledge that life's good and bad moments happen concurrently sometimes. Positive and negative markers in life happen back to back. We're on a rollercoaster of highs and lows. Occasionally there's a slow build-up and a quick drop. There might be an unexpected loop. At some point, the ride ends for all of us.

·♥·♥·♥·♥·♥·

Life is full of love. Life is full of loss. Life is full of heartbreak. Like in *Lesson One*, the letters in this section of With Love are particularly gut-wrenching but include honest accounts. Most of these letters are full of sadness, yet there is a search for learning and understanding in the moments of grief and loss. Some of the letters in this section reflect on the inevitable death of the individuals with whom the writers have complicated relationships. Letters may discuss the health, death, and dying process of a grandparent or parent. Other letters include a recollection of a slow deterioration of a friendship or romantic partnership.

In terms of human relationships, we may have friendships that come and go, we may get dumped, and we may do the dumping. We may experience some, none, or all of those relationship milestones. We grieve the ends of relationships in the way we grieve the end of our lives. In both cases, the people left behind must start anew. That scary feeling of being confronted by an unimaginable future that is without the individuals who were a significant presence in our lives is an inevitable part of our humanity.

Even the best relationships come to an end because every person has an expiry date. You have an expiration date. Your loved ones have an expiration date. Your greatest enemies have an expiration date. No one lives forever. These are the difficult moments you cannot escape. Knowing how little time we have left, however, consider how you want to spend these final years, months, days, and moments. Consider who you want to spend them with.

Lessons in the Key of Life - JP Rogers

Dear 20-year-old JP,

You'll barely be two decades old when you read this. Brace yourself for a hell of a ride! It's not for the faint of heart. You're going to lose and find yourself over and over again. And with each twist and turn, you won't be starting over. You'll be starting from experience. One of the hardest lessons you're going to learn is letting go. Life will show you contrast, like the black and white keys of a piano. It's going to be a constant balance of the good, the bad, and as a boyfriend once put it, "the dramatic." The piano will become your first major attraction and over time, your constant companion.

Seeing your reflection in its glossed, ebony frame will feel like an extension of yourself. You'll often recognize him more than the person staring back at you in the mirror every day. Every time you stray away it draws you back. It's going to give you a career. It will save your life many times. And when everything else comes and goes throughout your life, this wooden box of strings and hammers somehow always shows up at your door, comforting you in its ebony and ivory with roses in hand.

Life changes its beat when you least expect it. Staggering like the varying tempo of a deeply emotional Chopin nocturne. Layered as the harmonies of Stevie Wonder's *Innervisions*. Your life will have moments of beaming color against absolute darkness, just as a symphony modulates between major and minor keys. There will be times you'll never get the closure you desperately need. Many parts of your life will seem like unresolved cadences. I want to remind you that even through your most difficult times, your coda is still unwritten, and the best is yet to come.

Your spirit will grow with every win and loss. Each taste of heartbreak will feel like dying over and over again. There will be periods of your life filled with intense grief, depression, hopelessness and crippling anxiety. It'll feel like there's no seeing or living beyond it. In time, you realize that you have no choice but to accept and make peace with it. You learn to sit with it and befriend it. For so long you will not be ok and you wonder if you ever will be again. I'm here to tell you to hang on. Hang on tightly. You will be more than ok.

You're going to make a new life for yourself at 22, 28, and even into your 30s! You'll visit faraway places and reach highs that numb the pain of your past. You'll crash to lows that rob your will to live. All of it becomes part of your journey. You'll never fully understand its destination and you'll mostly travel alone with no compass. Despite the many bumps in the road, keep riding the waves. I need you to remain determined and emerge on the other side where peace, acceptance, and happiness wait to greet you with open arms.

As children, we accept the reality that's handed to us. You accept your given American name. You don't question why someone is "Asian" or why your parents only mark "White" in those little boxes. You accept what you are based on what you're told, but you also understand that part of you is not. Mom talks on the phone in a language you don't speak. You pick up a few phrases, but this aspect of you largely remains a mystery. You're given short answers and redirected when questioning them. You want to feel included, but you feel left out instead. Feeling left out was only a byproduct of what was quietly done for your best interest. If you were going to be successful in America, then you had to look like one, speak and write like one, and have a name like one.

Dealing with this becomes harder as you get older. You'll resent yourself and become angry as to why you lack a sense of identity. You'll continually feel alienated from your heritage, like a club you're not welcomed into. You aren't brown enough to be Filipino, and you're not white enough to be "White-non-Hispanic." Not to mention that awful acne all over your face. Oh yeah, and you'll be physically and emotionally attracted to men. Ugh. Looking in the mirror will make you confused. You don't even know who's looking back at you. That will all change though when you start a new life and a new love in Los Angeles, California. It'll be the beginning of a long road back to yourself. And one day you'll finally love yourself enough to just be...you. Speaking of a new life, make sure to pack an extra pair of shoes in your duffel bag. At 22 years old, you'll make one of the biggest moves of your life, and at a time when you least expect it.

Wanna know how LA welcomes you at 22?

Picture this. Day one of your new life in Cali: You step in the biggest pile of dog poop at a Filipino festival in San Pedro. But I don't blame you for being unprepared. Just the night before, you arrived on a flight wearing only the clothes on your back and a one-way ticket in hand. Before boarding that flight, you lived in a hotel for two weeks. It burned a hole in your heart (and your savings account). You'll be forcibly kicked out of your house and not allowed back in. You saw this coming though. Your parents were divorced. Your relationship with your mother was strained. She was not happy that you were gay and having a relationship with a man on the other side of the country. You were estranged from your father for years and resented him. You were also the one thing standing in their way of getting back together.

You were vilified by your family for being gay. You cried in the shower that morning and by that afternoon your cell phone service cut off at work. You came home and turned the key, only to find the door wouldn't open. A security door stop was propped against the knob from the inside. You're told you can't be here anymore. You lose everything. Your piano, your home, your family. Everything that you did not own was immediately disowned by you. The police were notified too, so when you ask for help, they turn you away. All you had at that moment was a pay phone, your boyfriend's number, and, luckily, your car keys to drive to a friend's house. The entire world was against you that night and the weeks to follow. You never felt so alone in your life, yet so free and liberated. Anxious and ready for a new start, one that would reunite your long-distance love, who is also your only lifeline at that time in your life.

I wish that feeling of ecstasy and reckless abandon could remain with you just a little longer. You'll soon learn that life is about to get a lot harder before it gets easier. Now he's asking for half of the rent– and all you have is a dwindling savings account and a cheap pay-as-you-go phone. You inherit all his friends and good times. But every Monday hits and you are all alone. Now you have to navigate a foreign city and find a job. And quickly. Feels like racing against a clock you can't outrun. Things aren't as rosy and adventurous as when you first visited each other. But the bond made during that long-distance struggle, and the longing shared for each other keep things from completely collapsing for now. But you're here living on their turf, on their terms, and nowhere to go if there is trouble. Fights will break out about things you didn't fight about before. There will be blow-ups and uncomfortable days, sometimes even weeks at a time without talking to each other. Just as you leave your old life behind, you're handed an even harsher reality check in this one.

28 gets dirty before 30.

The scariest feeling of your late twenties will be the moment you realize you're not happy or in love anymore. You'll start seeking love and affection elsewhere knowing very well it's wrong, but for a long time, you weren't stable enough to be on your own. Until now. It's still going to take a lot of courage to leave. One final ugly fight will draw the line in the sand. You're going to separate and make space to work things out. One day you'll sign a lease on an apartment with the intention of sharing weeknight dinners together. A few embattled exchanges will ensue and things suddenly start to become quiet. And no sooner than cutting the deposit, the cord is cut for good. You've just lost your boyfriend of eight years. The one who took you in when you were homeless and the one person who loved you more than the circumstances that defined you. You're now left with an empty apartment. Alone. Again. In a heartless and cruel city full of heartfelt memories you made together for almost a decade.

Your darkest days are ahead of you. You'll cry more than you'll smile and the world around you will feel so unfamiliar. You're going to drown in health problems and you'll lose the will to live. Your ability to carry out daily functions will be severely disrupted. You'll later learn that these debilitating symptoms are panic attacks. You'll enter a vicious cycle of medications and relapses that never seem to stabilize unless you up the milligram count. You'll harbor anger and bitterness over family trauma and it manifests into physical illness.

Hang on a little longer JP. Brighter days are still ahead. A few months later, a sweet, spunky pup named Canelo comes into your life. He gives you a reason to come home. Despite the ugly chaos within you, this pup just wants to hug you, kiss you, play with you, snuggle, and love you unconditionally. He gives you security and comfort. He makes your empty house a home. He's family. Every year gets a little easier. A sense of normalcy slowly returns. Hang on tight JP. It may seem like your world has fallen apart and there's no looking beyond it. But believe me when I say there's a whole new life beyond your heartbreak. You can't see it now, but you'll find a new way on your own. You're going to find a better job. You're also going to find love again and things will begin looking up. It's been so long since you were genuinely this happy and in love.

New decade, who dis?

You're still going to struggle to figure out who the hell you are and your place in the world as you enter your 30s. You had this clear picture of what a career in music and entertainment would look like for you, but no idea or any means of how to get there. Your first brush with rejection will be the time you sang a Barry Manilow song for your parents, hoping they would catch the hint and help you pursue show business. You're complimented but largely overlooked. Piano was "enough." Or the time they put you in modeling only to pull you out when offered a huge opportunity to sign and train with an agency in Atlanta. It wasn't in their "budget." You relied on them to believe in you, and they didn't meet your expectations. You'll feel like they failed you. You'll be told to get a regular job or "join the military, they'll give you a roof and a hot meal," pay your dues, do the minimum in life, and hopefully cross the finish line "comfortably."

You knew this wasn't for you. There's going to be a complete disconnect anytime you try to express your big dreams and aspirations to them. You're grateful for what you have, but you'll always demand and strive for more, and yet it's received as selfish. "Compared to what we had in the Philippines...you should be thankful for what you have." Okay, but you also left your country in search of a new life and new opportunities. You chose to raise your kids here in America. You should understand that more than anyone. This is a new generation in a capitalist culture, with different standards of what success should look and feel like to us. It's also been ten years and all I've amounted to is a whopping five grand in my emergency savings. I'd like to say that I've done more with my life besides working a day job and paying rent. "Well, you need to keep saving your money." I certainly try, but that's a bit difficult when the system is literally rigged to take everything from you. Sigh. You're going to have to figure this out on your own. It's going to be one of the hardest struggles you'll ever face, but damn it'll be so worth it.

Yeah, you could play the hell out of a piano, but you're growing tired of the same gigs, day in and day out, year after year. It goes nowhere. You're still working a dead-end job. Whenever you try auditioning for opportunities beyond your comfort zone, it always returns fruitless. Rejection sucks. Constant rejection hurts. You'll question why God gave you these skills and talents or even these huge aspirations, yet nowhere and nothing to use them for. You know you're capable of so much more. There will be so many close calls of pulling the plug, admitting to your parents that they were right, and crash landing back to a room in their house. Back to working your previous job at a supermarket for ten bucks an hour. Your hand is literally on the plug. But there's too much at stake. And your stubborn confidence always bailed you out. You know you can't give up and go back. That life was buried a long time ago. There's nothing there to go back to.

One day you come across a casting call on Instagram and you almost overlook it. One of your favorite Filipino vocal groups is LA-based and is casting a new choir to sing background on their new album, and also feature in the single's music video. This one felt close to home, and a chance to make some new friends and connections. Okay fine, one more audition tape. And this time you cut! Barely (lol). The video shoot quickly approaches and you don't hear anything back, just like every other audition you've done in the past. You have this moment of "see I told you so." But hey, let's just email and ask if you passed the audition. What do you have to lose, right? And to your surprise, the good news is returned, and you're so excited and grateful. Hmmm... should I have just emailed all my other auditions too?? (Haha). It's your first big break as a singer. This will be the start of something new and exciting for you. And yet, just a few days later, you're going to lose the love of your life. The man you were planning to marry.

He was supposed to be the one. The running joke was always "What am I gonna do with you?!" Sometimes out of comedic relief, oftentimes out of frustration, and with a witty grin, he'd always answer "Marry me" without skipping a beat. Just the night before, he sat starry-eyed across from you at his favorite Cuban restaurant. He gently held your hand on the table and assured you it'd just be a routine surgery, a short recovery and then we go home. Except we never got to go home.

You'll spend the next two weeks in the ICU and refuse to leave his side even for just a few hours. He's in a coma and needs you more than ever. You come very close to missing this video shoot altogether. Indecisive, you'll play the track in the car and learn your lines between drives to the hospital. You reluctantly decide to go, hoping it can comfort you and take your mind off of things, if only for a little bit. You show up to the gig, but all you can think about is him. In between takes you call to check on him and make sure he's still alive. You smile and sing your lines to the camera and no one has any idea what's going on inside of you.

It will take two years to accept that the man you deeply loved with your entire being was lost the night he hemorrhaged. You actually began losing him the night he suffered a seizure in your bed. You actually began losing him even as your relationship grew stronger and closer in the months to come. You'll lose him with each guided walk down the hallways of the rehabilitation center. You'll lose him a little more with every fight against his family to get access to him. You'll do everything in your power to save him, but nothing will bring back the man you once knew.

Not only do you lose him, but you're going to lose yourself in the process. You'll desperately try to hang on to what was, but when it's time to let go, it's time. Nothing will ever stop destiny. The forces that move these timelines are beyond your control. A long, spiraling vortex of grief and healing lies ahead. As heartbreaking as this was and continues to be, please know that it was necessary and inevitable.

During this time, you're going to reconcile with your parents again. As a grown man in your 30s with some of your own lived (and painful) experiences, you slowly come to see that you have a lot in common and that they've always been there for you all along. They may not have provided everything you expected to fulfill your needs or to achieve your dreams, but they love you deeply in the best way that only they know how. They stand ready to protect you and will spare no expense to help you.

Quite the plot twist, wasn't it? I know it's not what you wanted to hear. But these are some tough pills you'll have to swallow moving forward.

Stop the blame game and stop victim playing. It only traps you in a holding pattern of grief and anger. You need to make peace with this and acknowledge that your parents are more than enough. They are cheering you on and they are proud of you, contrary to your belief. They worry for your well-being as parents always will. Just show them that you got this. And don't be too prideful to ask for their help or advice. Their wisdom and insight exceed your limitations in this world, and you need them.

Accept people where they are. Stop trying to change people. Change how you deal with them whether it's friends, colleagues, partners, or even your parents. The people that are meant to stay in your life will stay. When things have run their course, allow it to go. Stop controlling situations and outcomes. This will be your ultimate undoing. You did the best you could with what you knew at the time. And you'd do it all over again for the ones you love. But know when it's time to let go. Don't rely on others to make you happy. Make yourself happy. Healing will never be linear. Establish boundaries to protect your peace. Be gentle on days that feel harder than others. Okay, so today was a shitshow. So what? It is what it is. Tomorrow is a new day. It's okay to not be okay once in a while.

Use this time to get to know yourself again. You are deserving of all that you dream and desire. You have yet to meet all the people who will love and celebrate you for who you are, just the way you are. Put yourself first again. Take responsibility for yourself and watch a new level unlock in this game. What lessons have you learned from it all? Acknowledge and follow the synchronicities you've been seeing. Don't chase, but instead attract what you want to become by being it NOW. And when you're ready, go out there and conquer. Life begins at the end of your comfort zone. The life you want lies just beyond all of your fears and insecurities.

Cherish love in its present moment. Reciprocate and never take it for granted. You never know when it can be taken from you. And it was, in the blink of an eye. If there's one thing you want people to know, it's that selfless acts of love know no bounds. Being gay does not preclude one from experiencing love. The notion that you are not loved or worthy of love because you are gay is nothing more than a paradigm. Your heart's capacity to love is actually limitless in the eyes of the divine. We are all equally capable of giving and receiving it, and you're not some lesser of a human being for deeply loving a person of the same sex. Love is a frequency, not a condition. It would never discriminate or turn its back on you. Don't let the world harden your heart because it hurts you. Love also teaches you very hard lessons, because that's the only way for you to grow, and to understand how to love better. Know your boundaries, but always remember to lead with love.

Know that I am with you as you continue forward and face the unknown. Trust the process. You are exactly where you're meant to be. You were never late, you were never lacking, you were always right on time. Strike the first notes of your new song. Let each cadence resolve with hope and determination. Life is not what happens to you, but what happens FOR you. How do you respond to it? Love yourself again, JP. No one can do that better than YOU. And no matter what, don't ever give up. All the chips will fall into place thereafter. You'll see. Your coda is still unwritten. Now go get 'em champ.

With deepest love for you
(and cheering you on),
JP at 35

SALTED - GABRIELLA BUBA

Dear Younger Me,

I know Grandmother feels like she's been old forever, but now the weight of it is gathering in her bones, making them brittle and her skin thin. She's lost sight in one eye. She falls too often. She's a hard woman, who lived a hard life, who loves hard and hurts hard. It's the way she was raised. There was no other way for women like her.

The way she hurls the word FAGGOT burns like salt in a wound you don't remember receiving. Like the salt she can no longer see pouring fast, turning her pot of ginger chicken lugaw inedible. Hold her hand gently anyway. Add in the day-old rice and a splash of vinegar, to save the pot.

Drive her where she needs to go, now that they've taken her license. Like when she always picked you up after school. Dig the garden this year. Deeper, deeper, push the hurt down with inedible table scraps into the soil for richness, fish bones and discarded rinds will feed sprouted seeds: Mango, calamansi, and papaya. And flowers. So many flowers: Hibiscus, oleander, orchids, and plumeria. Grandma plants flowers and fruit, and black sticking mud becomes bounty and beauty. It feels like she's always been with you, but she won't be with you long.

You will remember the salt-tart richness of green mango and bagoong from her garden longer than her slurs.

With Love,
Gabriella Buba

Old Wounds - Francis Joseph J. Gallego

You never knew this day would come, even at 35 years old.

You have already lived hundreds of lifetimes, and I know how hard it is to be in your dad's house right now. The Philippines has always been such a complex place for you; a place where you spent some of your hardest years and where your pain was born.

I know that this is the second time back in the Philippines and the last time you saw or spoke to your dad is when you came out to him, and he flipped the fucked out and disowned your brown ass. Your father has always been this tall, scary, man; with skin as dark as night, who can move the world with his tongue or anger.

Fuck. Now, look at you; choosing to be with him in his final days. You're either fucking crazy, or *hella* brave, but I am proud of you. You have done so much healing to be in this moment and face your boogeyman.

I know that you have never been able to be authentically yourself in the Philippines, and this has caused a lot of fucking disconnection to your Filipino culture and sense of self. I know you wish your dad did a better job in raising you and your brother George, but maybe his biggest gift was not raising you and George at all; because you and George would have turned out to be sociopaths.

I also know that this is so confusing and painful; having to manage not just your emotions, but your mother's and your brother's, as well as the trauma that they have experienced. I know that you will continue to find healing, authenticity, truth, and healthy love with and from your chosen and biological families. You are continuing to heal your fractured and wounded hearts.

Remember this and wear it on your heart and soul: *Someone's inability to love or celebrate your authentic self is a reflection of them and their inability to love themselves; it has nothing to do with you.*

Welcome home; you deserve to fucking be here.

You deserve loving kindness,
Francis

No One Talks About the Best Friend Breakup - Jeff Deguia

Dear early summer 2023 Jeff,

This summer has been filled with surprises and not necessarily the ones you celebrate. Over the years, the conversation of the chosen family has come front and center among young people, but especially with young queer people. You've been here in California for 11 years and you've been so fortunate to meet great people, form friendships, and find and build your chosen family.

I could have never imagined having to end a friendship, especially with a very important best friend. It's been a summer filled with a heartbreak you never thought you would experience. But here we are, life just panned out this way. It rocked your world in the worst way. You've cried so many tears, sadness has filled your veins, and anger has been mixed in.

No one talks about best friend breakups. No one talks about how unbearable and how difficult they are. I never thought about what my life could look like without him in it, he was supposed to be in my life forever and I imagined him in all my future big life moments. But the pain of what happened is much stronger than the pain of him not being in my life.

I know it feels like we're losing so much, but we know what our boundaries are and we know what to expect from people we consider family. We deserve to be treated with respect, honesty, and love and that was not what happened.

I'm writing to a version of myself that is so recent, but I write to tell you that it's going to be okay. I can't say *when* it will be or *how* it will be, but instead, we are building confidence every day as we try to navigate through this pain. It's become easier to advocate for myself over the years because of therapy. But in this situation, even with that knowledge, it was still difficult to decide because I didn't think we would ever be here.

I promise in time things will get better and remind you that nothing in life is truly final. You didn't rule out a reunion. But we know right now, we do not want him in our life. I remind you that you can love someone from a distance and can honor a profound and memorable friendship that once was. This time is for us to heal, to love ourselves, and to grow through this unexpected change.

Summer 2023 Jeff, I remind you that loving yourself and setting your bound-aries is for you and you only. You get to call the shots in your life. People will have opinions, but the only one that matters is yours. It's your life and you get to live it on your terms.

Things will get better; be patient with yourself and give it time. Take this time to love you. You deserve it.

All the love in the world,
Jeff

Don't Wait - Mary Sabino

Dear Me,

Don't wait. You'll tell yourself for years that waiting to come out to your family will be easier once your grandparents have left Earthside. You'll tell yourself that you are sparing them the grief, prayers, and judgment from others that they may encounter, especially in their Catholic community. You'll tell yourself that it will be easier this way because their generation just grew up in a different time and you don't know what you'll do if they don't accept you.

Don't listen to these thoughts. This way of thinking will rob you of the joy and love that you deserve because at the end of the day, you will still be theirs and their hearts will remain the same for you. Give them the chance to love you as you are before it's too late.

With Love,
Mary

O Meets H - O. Ayes

O,

Where do I begin? It has been over two decades since I embarked on a life that would lead to deeper, truer happiness, despite societal and familial expectations, despite heart-wrenching situations a more logical person would avoid. Tomorrow night, you will go out to a lesbian bar with your *pinsan*, who isn't really related to you but your parents knew each other as children, so you are almost like family. Your sister and her husband would refer to him as "*Gay* E." You have another one of your many arguments about prejudices. They insist: "There's nothing wrong with that. It's just like saying, '*Mr.* B'."

Your *pinsan* is dressed in a tight-jean jumpsuit, reminiscent of JLO, with a wig, and you are in a black, one-strap dress and heels. In this lesbian bar, you are a target. Older women drinking beer turn their heads, but you continue as normal–dancing and laughing with your *pinsan* and his friends, trying not to give fag-hagish vibes.

Soon, you take interest in a tall woman, who has short, loose, brown curls and a white tank top with baggy jeans. You sit by her and ask her name. "H". But she gives you a mean look and ignores you for a while. You keep sitting nearby and try to look unfazed. You hate techno so you are not dancing. Because she looks slightly Hispanic, you ask about her background and she tells you that she is as "white as can be," but later clarifies that she has Italian ancestry.

After a while, she decides you are not a threat, and for the next hour, there is a real conversation: Where you both graduated high school, that she wants to major in psychology at a community college, that her parents have moved to Florida to help her younger sister try to make it as a professional tennis player. You learn that she lives on her own in South City, where you will be moving soon too, because you have had enough of your sister's husband and being their unpaid nanny.

You and H dance together, but it is time to go. You ask without hesitating, "Can I have your number?"

"I was just going to ask you that." Later, you learn that she already gave her number to your *pinsan*, to give to you later. You are over the moon. This first night, you would not tell her about your on-again, off-again boyfriend who is in the Army, stationed in Hawaii. You had already decided before tonight that the next time he calls–who knows when that will be–you'll break up with him. You would tell H about him a few days later, and she understands your intention to break it off.

Over the next weeks, you explore what it is like in this alternate universe where you are no longer the heterosexual norm. It feels like being a pre-teen again, heart skipping when she sends a message, talking for hours on the phone at night. On second thought, you were never that way with boys. When she kisses you for the first time, after watching a movie on the couch, you have never felt so *free*.

"I'm sorry, but I couldn't wait," she tells you, sweetly. You are still waiting on that phone call from Hawaii.

"I'm glad you couldn't. I want to be with you."

You get to know her beautiful body, how to make her squirm and gasp in pleasure. You learn about your own body, how – despite your feelings for her, how she turns you on as she kisses you all over – you are not able to feel safe enough to let go. You wonder if this discomfort has anything to do with her, or if you are just too guarded. You think about the only person to have ever made you let go – the boy in Hawaii –and feel instantly guilty.

One evening, you notice a scar on her wrist, which she says is "nothing." You feel her pull away. You both lie there in silence, unable to hold each other. You recall the story of her ex, "S", who tore H's heart into barely salvageable pieces. S was with a man previously and left H for another man. You make a promise to yourself that you will not do that to H. Ever.

"I'm worried you will leave me and go back to your ex. I also don't know if I should stay in this city. Before I met you, I was going to leave for Florida since the lease on my apartment was up. Come with me."

"Or you can stay and move in with me." She is ecstatic and so are you. You find out later about that U-Haul joke. You hate being a stereotype, but you go with it.

You wish with all your heart that this love story has a happy ending. Your first girl love. Except, merely a week later, as you are trying to clean the dusty tops of the kitchen cabinets, she comes home with another decision: "I want to be single, get lost in a book, do whatever I want. I don't want to think about another person. I'm not ready to be in a relationship."

You don't try to convince her otherwise. "I want you to be happy." You don't realize what heartbreak feels like until she has already moved out and you are left alone in the apartment. You do not sob, but you feel an emptiness sink deep into your chest.

You cannot call your friends to console you. They do not understand your new life, how all of a sudden you are someone different who may end up being attracted to one of them. You seek out instead, the attention given to you by another woman you met – "M". You do not know that your broken heart will ignore the red flags, the lies, until it is almost too late.

It will take you years to recover, at least just enough to love again and again and again. Do not give up. One day, a woman will love you in a way you have always deserved.

With Love,
O (2023)

LESSON TEN

Unapologetically take up space.

I was formerly the Director of Curriculum and Instruction for a youth program, *Lakas Mentorship,* which supported young Filipino Americans in the Inland Empire, Orange County, as well as Los Angeles County of southern California. Part of my role included the development of programming that would encourage leadership development, ethnic identity development, and mentorship of high school and college-level Filipino-American students. Some community expectations that were often called upon included the following:

Take space.

Make space.

Safe space.

These are terms I have heard and used in other spaces in the context of Diversity, Equity, Inclusion, and Justice forums in professional and academic environments. This framework of *take space, make space,* and *safe space* is a wonderful map that shows me, as a queer Filipino, how to interact with others and the environment around me. This is true regardless of whether I am an engaging facilitator or a shy participant.

Take space encourages folks to communicate freely and to assert their ideas without fear. To *make space* is to step aside to allow others to participate in the discussion without disruption. And *safe space* is a condition we must uphold in the space we occupy; it ensures that the conversations and group remain inclusive and welcoming. In tandem, these three phrases are a framework in which leaders and community members can facilitate critical and meaningful conversations that benefit ourselves and the group as a whole.

I like to keep these phrases in mind especially when working with groups that often exist in the margins. Take space, make space, and safe space are necessary reminders that help marginalized groups unlearn this false notion that they do not belong.

You do in fact belong.

As a queer Filipino, you belong.

We are too often *making space* for others outside of our own community.

Marginalized folks, such as queer Filipinos, are sometimes conditioned to believe that they must shrink themselves to make room for those who *actually* belong or who have authority. It is deep within the subconscious. Marginalized communities may find themselves defaulting to being the quietest in the room, to stepping out of the way for others to step in front, to waiting until spoken to before speaking up, to grinning and bearing their pain, to leading requests with apologies.

It's a beautiful and kind thing to make space for others, but as queer Filipinos, we could do so much more by unapologetically taking up space.

Queer Filipinos are often forced out of spaces or made to feel like they do not belong. Safe spaces specifically for queer Filipinos are hard to come by. Even more difficult is the task of making space for other queer Filipinos when we feel powerless and oppressed. Because we continue to be a highly marginalized community, I strongly believe that we must *take space*, first and foremost. When we stand up to take space in settings that are not built for queer Filipinos, we become more visible, and in turn, our own perspectives and feelings about decisions that inadvertently or directly impact us will suddenly matter more. When we have given representation to others within our community by *taking space*, we *make space* for them and future generations to step in and do the same. When we queer Filipinos take space in environments that need us, we will make space for our community to show themselves, which in effect will create a safe space for all. Hopefully, the cycle continues.

·♥·♥·♥·♥·♥·

We have reached the final set of letters contributed to With Love. These are the last of this project, but they are certainly not the least. I did want to end here though because if there's any one thing I hope you will take from this experience it's this. Take up space...and don't be sorry for it. The letters in this chapter talk about making bold choices, feeling empowered, and encouraging independent critical thought. These writers embrace the attributes they bring to the table and encourage others to recognize that everyone has their own unique strengths.

FASHION FORWARD – RESI IBAÑEZ

Hello, human.

This is the Magic 8 ball speaking, the one your Tito Angelito got you for Christmas. What he didn't tell you is that I've been sitting in a closet for the past few years, just waiting to be given away to some human as a gift. And here I am now in your hands.

You may be too young now to understand the significance of the closet. Right now, I know the favorite things you have in your closet are a red dress with white polka dots (Minnie Mouse style) and a holiday dress with a black velvet top, a green crepe skirt, and a shiny silver pin on the waistband.

Grown-ups around you know what *a closet* means. It's where people hide things. Secrets they don't want other people to know. And most often the people who hide things in closets are people like you– but you don't know that yet.

What you do know is that you hate the distinctions between "boys" things and "girls" things. When you ask your mom what the difference is between boys and girls, you don't believe her. *That can't be right,* you think. *It seems like people make such a big deal about the difference between boys and girls. Boys and girls have different clothes and toys and are treated differently .... And it's all just because of body parts? That doesn't seem right.*

Years later, you get wise to *the closet* as a metaphor for something to hide. But I came from the closet. And I'm not your typical Magic 8 ball.

I spent a lot of time observing your Tito Angelito. What he kept in his closet, how he didn't always dress in men's clothes. I've developed a keen eye for fashion and became a Magic 8 Fashion ball.

I can tell you what you'll keep in your closet as you get older. How you think you might have some secrets, but your clothes say otherwise. *In the closet* is a metaphor for hiding. But what you have in your closet tells a different story.

2001 - 2004. The green army-style jacket from the sales rack in the gap kids boys' section from the first day you leave Catholic school uniforms for seventh grade in public school. The thick-soled boots will make you taller and everyone can hear as you make your entrance. Your keychain with a picture of Sporty Spice. Denim overalls paired with a fringed belt. Flared jeans with bleached-out ankle-length spots and rhinestones on the hem. Studded belt from Hot Topic.

Black and pink Vans sneakers from the factory outlet store. The oversized blue and yellow rugby shirt that was a hand-me-down from Kuya Eric. The light blue crochet kerchief with a navy silk ribbon you will wear every day in the summer, on the way to go swimming with your bathing suit in a red Hello Kitty duffle bag. The first time you realize you could wear shorts with your bathing suit they will be red, orange, and yellow striped, a sunset. The black velour ankle length skirt with silver glitter flowers on the hem you'll wear to your first dance at public school. The eternal desire for cargo pants. The denim jacket with a floral pattern circa 1998 from American Girl will miraculously still fit you twenty years later, and the pink scrunchie in the pocket. Your red Walkman. Red and brown beaded necklace with a floral pendant from Claire's. Black t-shirt with a Keith Haring heart print.

2007 - 2018. The red scalloped dress with a built-in corset that you'll get on discount for $99 for prom. The gold jewelry and shawl from the consignment shop, the salon ladies who are your mom's friends pronouncing *ay que linda* when they finish doing your hair. The full tuxedo you'll rent from Keezers for a wedding, with a gray top hat the bride's grandfather will steal to wear on the dance floor. Black fake leather boots with silver studs and buckles. The secondhand leather jacket that was a tad too small, that will come after you have the dream where an older queer calls you the *Butch of Ives Street*. The yellow flower hair clip your mom will give you for college graduation, you'll wear pinned to the mortarboard. Secondhand black vest with a fake suede front. The navy blue high-waisted linen pants with suspenders make you look like Annie Hall. Painted on hand-me-down mom jeans, with green and blue, purple, and white acrylic splatter. The pink skirt you'll sew yourself with pattern design shapes in beige, brown, and blue. Your first binder will be navy blue. Your first pair of boxers will be purple and gray striped. Chaotic black overalls with pastel line drawings. The gray button-down from the Old Navy men's section with a moon-phase printed pattern that will be the only shirt you'll have for Mom's funeral.

2018 - 2019. The R initial pin you'll find in Nanay's jewelry box, three generations of Ibañezes carrying this letter. The gold filigree necklace from the 1950s or 1960s, or maybe earlier, is shaped by an indigenous platero in Benguet or Ilocos, delicately molding hot precious metal. Forging the ongoing story of resistance to the Spanish who wanted control of the gold veins in the northern mountains, but who could not conquer the land, the people. The barong Tagalog from your wedding to your wife is made from pineapple fibers, woven, sewed, and embroidered by hand in the Philippines. Shimmery, iridescent, like sunlight. The black pants from JC Penney magically did not need any alteration. White and gold felt flower headband, custom-designed was done gold Converse. The makeup done by a trans woman artist at Sephora, who will say *this is what the world needs. More people are loving on each other. More love.* The big gold hoop earrings.

Human, keep being you, wearing what *you* want. You have nothing to keep closeted. But I do enjoy your fashion choices.

The hand-me-down
Magic 8 Fashion Ball
who sees you for you

STAY YOU, ALWAYS - LJ BALAJADIA

Dear LJ,

Yes, it's me from the future, spooky, right? If you're looking for me to spoil the future for you, I won't do that, unfortunately. Instead, I'm here to offer some choice words to you: Things you should keep in mind and know as you navigate the next few years before you get to my position. However, I will say, that you are going to get to see one of your teenage idols, on tour, twice, bawling your eyes out when you hear your favorite song live.

First off, welcome to *kind of* accepting the fact that you're not straight! Congratulations! I wish I could throw a party for you with cake and balloons, but that's not how it's going to work. People are going to tell you that you need to do X to be able to do Y, and while some of the things they say are true... please, take the time to figure things out on your own. While the world can accept you hiding yourself or being a version of yourself that better fits what everyone else wants or expects you to be, the world should not accept you being comfortable with not being yourself or being whatever image of what they want you to be. You should be unapologetically you and tell everyone else to "deal with it" [old habits die hard, I guess, you'll cringe at this later]. Wear the clothes you want, grow out your hair, shave it, and make sure to go to the gym every once in a while!

You're going to get hurt, a lot. You'll be hurt by people you think you love and by people who you think love you. And while I could tell you to "fuck the haters" and "just do you," instead, I'm telling you to go all out and love those people and learn from them as much as possible. You get to see your friends have relationships in high school and college and grow and mess up and you didn't get that. It doesn't help that you're the token gay in all of your friend groups.

Sure, the first guy you make out with might have to teach you how to use your tongue, and your first big relationship might end up with you isolated from your friends. But, that's okay. Your real friends will be there when you crawl out of that relationship and you'll instead have this unwavering faith in good character and falling in love. You deserve that.

Last, throughout this, I want to say that you are not a person in the background nor a supporting character! You can imagine yourself to be the main character of a story. People will care about what happens to you and what you say or do. People will miss you even when you don't feel like they will. People will love you even when you feel like you cannot and will not love yourself. And more importantly, you are responsible for everything that happens to you and can feel what you feel without remorse. I know what you've felt, know what you will feel, and again, I can't say it's going to be "sunshine and rainbows" as much as you want it to be, but you'll be okay.

Enjoy being yourself and don't let the world tell you "no" without a fight! You're going to put up with more bullshit than you can count. And someday, when you get to where I am, writing this letter, I hope you have more profound things to tell your younger self.

Love,
Older LJ

Dear Black Sheep - Joel Baker

Letter to my teenage self:

Teenage Me. Stop calling yourself bisexual (you never connected with that word) and stop hating on relationships. You will eventually figure this out scrolling on *Tumblr* but I will just save you some time. You are pansexual. And polyamorous. You will have periods or phases of exploration in sex and in drag, of homophobia, misogyny, misandry, and finally full acceptance of yourself and others. Your journey of gender identity and sexuality as well as your views on relationship and love will be a rollercoaster for sure but it will all be worth it. Trust.

My adopted definition of *pansexual* is that love is love and attraction is attraction. Pansexuality means that a connection is not just romantic or sexual; it is fluid. You can have any type of connection between you and another person. The experience can be dynamic, intimate, or carnal. This is regardless of race or gender. *Polyamory,* to some people, is to simply be non-monogamous. But to me it means freedom for you and your partner(s); you do not possess each other's bodies, you do not police each other's choices and you don't judge each other's feelings. You support and love each other as best friends and teammates without being slaves to each other.

Oh, and your preferred gender pronouns are he/him/her/she/they/them (not ze/zir; no offense).

Ok, now the deep shit. Being in a Filipino family means they won't understand you. They are gay and straight. They will call you half-half. That's what they call bisexual, even though the truth ain't that clean. Your mom is going to find your drag outfit, your wig and dress, and heels, and cry hysterically screaming, "Nooooo my son is *baklaaaa,* oh noooo." She'll blame herself for buying girl toys as well as Ninja Turtles and Power Rangers when you were a kid. For letting you sing Spice Girls and learn the choreography of Britney Spears, even though you had crushes on those female pop stars as well (bi panic). Why is it "alternative" and taboo and "wrong" to explore your identity? And even worse, to find out you are different? And is the LGBTQIA+ community welcoming with open arms to the outcast? Not always. It's a war. Gays vs straights; and being bisexual or pan means you are not choosing a side. But maybe that's on to something, while I want there to be more than two sides and there not to be a war between them, maybe for peace, there needs to be war first. For them to understand me, maybe I have to argue to make them listen.

When I first thought about writing this letter, I thought there was nothing I really wanted to tell you because I don't regret anything (except college debt) and I wouldn't want to influence or change what will make you the person I am now, who I love and fully accept. But there is advice: Don't stop fighting. Don't stop being different. Don't give into "tradition," don't conform just to make the family happy. Your sister and your cousin may be lesbians, and you may bond with them and be misandrist for a time, but they still will not really relate to you being mostly male passing and your unique struggles as a cis, pansexual, polyamorous male. You are really on your own. You can and should have their back and fight for their struggles to be known and heard as well (you are an intersectional feminist and need to be an ally in the feminine fight and struggles). But only you can share your story and how you, specifically, identify. Get people to hear it, and they *do* need to hear it.

Progress and fighting prejudice come from representation and getting people to see what is different from them; getting them to really see it and accept it. Also, we need to destigmatize these "alternative" views and lifestyles. Freedom comes from choice and options. To give the option to be *polyam* or *pan.* Heterosexuality, the gender binary, and monogamy aren't the default; just one option of many. That's the fight you are supposed to fight. Don't be a sheep. Don't conform.

You will get burnt out and water yourself down, but just dust off the char, dry off the water, and get back in the ring. Yes, try to do everything with the intention of love, but sometimes you need to show *tough love* and sometimes love isn't the beneficial action; it's painting the town red and breathing fire. Own yourself, love yourself, and don't let other voices make you feel or think any differently. Spread love through understanding others and through prying open the closed-minded. The status quo only wins because of the *bandwagon effect*: They have numbers. But just stand your ground and when the going gets tough, just read this letter again and know you are who you are supposed to be. No one can tell you differently. Grow in yourself, water yourself, and learn about yourself and others. But the real takeaway here is to choose sides. Those sides are intersectional feminism, the LGBTQIA+ community, and ultimately yourself and your story.

Be an activist and fight,
Big Joel

BAKLA BISAYAN-NESS - SEAN-JOSEPH TAKEO KAHᴀOKALANI CHOO

Dear Eighteen-Year-Old Me,

First of all, let's get the obvious out of the way: sex, intimacy, preferences, all of that jazz; it's a big *halo-halo* mess...but that's okay. Life sometimes is a big *halo-halo* mess. It can be confusing and overwhelming, but it can also be good. The feelings you feel and how they differ from those around you isn't necessarily a bad thing: You know this; you're weird. It's a strength. You like being different, unique, off-kilter. Being queer is just another unique quality of yours.

So own your *weird*.

So, I'm 34 right now, just about twice your age. And you are in a huge transition time in your life. I don't think you can appreciate it (or handle it) at this time, but this late teens/early twenties time in your existence is probably one of the most bumpy stages of our life. You'll have other crazy relationships like the one you are in now (not as conflict-ridden, but still emotionally taxing, because you extraaaaaa, and you pick out *dramalani* queens to date sometimes). They will all be periods of growth and learning (I know you hate to label relationships as points of learning, but it's true) for yourself and your exes. And it's hard, and it's exhausting, and it's depressing, but it's all maturing you. So, that's good. The more you are willing to confront conflict sooner than later, the braver and wiser you become, like Link, solving a puzzle.

So also own your challenges.

You're falling in love with the performing arts right now, especially singing, and acting. It feels powerful, right? To have your voice heard, to charm others onstage, yeah? Enjoy it: Just don't abuse that power. I know you won't, but you're in college, and you're getting cocky, so don't let your skills get to your head. And I know you're conflicted about whether you should pursue music or theater, it's not an either/or thing. You have so many experiences waiting for you, playing gigs, recording albums, touring children's theater, working in both the West Coast and East Coast (yes, NYC) doing all sorts of cool stuff, meeting all sorts of awesome people, using both your musical background and your newfound passion for the theater. And guess what? There are a lot of other cool people out there who are queer, part-Filipino, and who were brought up Catholic. You're not alone. And they are writing about their experiences. You write about your experiences, and you win awards with the plays you write with your specifically queer Fil-Am lens.

So own your *Bakla Bisayan-ness.*

Speaking of *baklas*, I don't think you really know much about this, but your Uncle Duque's stage name was *Sean Duque*. And he wrote songs, and performed, like you. He traveled the world de-stigmatizing AIDS and thus humanizing and dignifying people living with AIDS until he succumbed to that disease. He helped his cousins out on their journey in queerness too. And from the beyond, he's going to help you too. You should ask your Uncle Kaholo...I mean, Uncle Butch about him. Why are there so many nicknames in our culture? Anyway, you should ask your Uncle Butch/Kaholo/Joseph Jr. about your Filipino side! He knows a lot.

By the way, I know it's uncomfortable to talk about some of these things, but no shame! You have cousins who are queer. Also, speaking of family/shame/faith, it's possible to have spirituality and queerness live next to each other, it just has never been really modeled for you.

So own your intersectionality-ees.

I hope you learn to prioritize your healing and your needs over others, sooner than later. I hope you learn to trust your *na'au*, trust your gut, and learn to trust your instincts. And I hope I can hear from you someday. That would be cool.

Love,
Sean

YOUR BIGGEST FAN - AJ JOHNSON

Oh little AJ,

You precious, feisty little thing.

How I wish that someone was there for you to stoke that fire in your spirit. That fire that, at 4 years old, made you argue with your mother when she told you that you had to start wearing a shirt outside because you saw that your neighbor's dad was shirtless outside all the time.

You were right, dear one, to question the arbitrary rules that were assigned to you because you were named, "girl."

How I wish I could spare you from so much of the pain you feel from awkwardly trying to perform femininity because that is what you were told to do to be liked and accepted.

How I wish that someone might have helped you dislodge the identity of *female* a bit earlier, and I wonder if maybe that would have been enough to disrupt the process of desperately chasing the validation from boys to affirm you.

How I wish I could have gifted you the freedom that lies outside of the male gaze sooner so that you might step into the magic of your sovereignty younger.

But even though there was nobody there to hold you in your defiance and even though you did not have the words *butch*, *queer*, or *nonbinary*, you never quite succumbed to the pervasive training into the subjugation that the patriarchy demanded of you as a young AFAB person.

You were taught, at every turn, to be as small as possible – both physically and emotionally. You were handed the tools that we hand everyone who is to grow into what we have defined as "woman," in this world: People-pleasing, compliance, deferring to others, avoiding at all costs burdening others, staying out of the way, not having any desires or needs, not having any opinions or a voice at all. And yet, you could not make your spirit that small.

You found a way to keep that fire burning, you brave and beautiful soul.

Thank you for tending to it for us.

Thank you for fighting until I had the words to name the shackles of the good-girl-conditioning that bound us until I had the strength to unlock those restraints.

Thank you for never forgetting that we were not born to be convenient.

You precious, feisty little thing.

Thank you for continuing to drive me to unlearn all of this bullshit, to permit us to take up space unapologetically, to own our power even if that makes waves. Thank you for continuing to inspire me to cause good and necessary trouble in a world that does not want us to be free.

Your biggest fan,
Big AJ

Spaces Do Nothing - Harlee Castro Balajadia

To the one looking for space,

When you think about it, a space by itself isn't really safe. Because a space when you're alone leaves you to spiral to who knows what. But you know what you being in that room alone does for someone else? It allows *them* to share that space with you. It allows *you* to share it with them. It allows the space to do what it does best.

Hold you.

It allows you the space to practice, to navigate, to feel, to express, to communicate, to love. Because you were brave enough to be in that room, you were able to create that space for at least one other person to share their story and their journey with you. And see that's the amazing thing about you.

A space alone isn't safe. *It's safe people who create safe spaces.*

Because of you – so many people in the world are equipped with the skills to share that safety with other people.

Because of you – you're able to see how safe you are with the conversations and words you've exchanged with the world around you.

Because of you – someone's world changed from meaning nothing... to meaning everything. And...

Because of you, you're able to be yourself. The only version – the one and only person that can be that person for others.

The beauty of leading with warmth, love, and acceptance is knowing that without any materials, products, or resources – you can create a *safe* space. A *loving* space to so many people. A space is a blank canvas – leaving every moment to have an infinite amount of possibilities that can shift realities for an infinite amount of people. Thank you for sharing the space. You have no idea how many people you'll change over the years.

With Love,
Your Current Self

The Softest, Sweetest, and Most Queer Love Letter - Ron Blakely

Dear little RC,

It's okay to take up space. It's okay to speak your mind because what you have to say is valuable. I'm sorry that you often felt like that wasn't true—that you were so fearful of making a mistake or saying the wrong thing or coming off as a little "too soft" that you often didn't do or say anything at all. "Keep quiet, lay low, don't rock the boat." That was really stifling. One day you'll know it. One day you'll understand that whatever narrative you were feeding into that told you to be quiet, to hide, to feel shame... is a lie. The truth is that you need to be seen, you need to be heard, and you deserve to be loud about it. Let the softest, sweetest, and most queer parts of you set you apart, but also give you a sense of belonging. One day you'll see it. One day you'll recognize the value of your presence—that many people take comfort in the warmth, ease, and kindness you bring into a room. Others will see the softest, sweetest, and most queer parts of you and call them beautiful. You are so loved, and the more you lean into how true that is, the more you'll see its evidence. It'll take many more years of hiding and dimming, and even self-hatred for you to realize this. I'm sorry that you ever felt like you needed to disappear.

One day you'll feel it. One day you're gonna love yourself—boldly. You're still learning what that fully means, but you'll look at the softest, sweetest, most queer parts of yourself and call them beautiful. The journey is already happening for you. You'll look back on it proudly. Today, you are the happiest and most yourself you've ever felt, knowing that there's still so much left to learn and love. Know that getting there does not come easy and that you will suffer many more years of heartache and deep loss—the kind that numbs. But know that you will make it on the other side of that more fortified, compassionate, authentic, and sure of yourself than ever before. Life's ups and downs become beautiful as you begin to see the purpose in everything. Take one day at a time, little RC. Give those beautiful parts of yourself the warmest hugs. Get to know them; see them—really see them; And love them in the softest, sweetest, and most queer way. I'm really proud of how far you've come, and I'm excited about where you're gonna go. I love you, kid.

Love always,
Ron

WHAT NOW?

Dear Reader,

Thank you for making it to the end of With Love.

With the help and support of an entire community, we set out to create a book to share what we wish we knew about being queer and Filipino in America. I'm proud to say that we did just that. After analyzing sixty-eight letters written by 50 queer Filipino Americans (as well as myself), common themes became apparent and were framed as these 10 distinct life lessons:

1. Life is hard. Forgive yourself.

2. Beware of perfectionism, people-pleasing, and self-depletion.

3. Be critical of your relationship to religion.

4. Your parents were doing what they knew. Take it or leave it.

5. Find your chosen family.

6. Break a few rules and have fun.

7. Media has the power to change lives.

8. Finding love and being loved is a damn journey.

9. You will experience loss and heartbreak.

10. Unapologetically take up space.

My hope is that With Love will uplift and educate others, especially the present and future queer Filipino Americans who pick up this book. It is important that this work exists as it is somewhat of a guide for other queer Filipinos to live as authentically and as joyfully as possible. This work should also remind others that queer Filipinos are woven into the fabric of American history, during a time when those who choose to erase queer perspectives by removing any trace of our experiences and ideas from literature and other media, the existence of this book at all is an act of resistance. I hope that means something to those who contributed their heartfelt letters and to those who are reading them at this very moment.

Amongst the queer Filipino community, there is immense diversity in attitudes towards life circumstances and perspectives of the world around us. I hope With Love has encouraged you to think long and hard about the world around you, so that you can make your own decisions about how to show up for yourself and for the folks who depend on you.

After reading to this point, you may have experienced a range of emotions. Relief, happiness, validation, sadness, anger, envy, and others. That's okay. Feel what you've got to feel. There may be several things in this book with which you disagree. I suspect there may have been parts of this book that made you feel uncomfortable or made you feel upset. Whatever that moment was for you, I would ask that you take a breather and reflect on why you felt such strong emotions.

> *Do your values align or conflict with the lessons gleaned from the letters contributed to this book?*
>
> *Do you have similar or different lived experiences and perspectives on the issues discussed in this book?*
>
> *Do you agree or disagree with the insights I've provided throughout this book?*
>
> *Do you have additional or alternative interpretations of the letters submitted to this book?*

Continue to consider these questions. Whatever your responses may be, they are absolutely valid. The most important piece here is that you think critically and independently to come to your own conclusions. You have your own lived experiences that are important and I thank you for taking the time to connect with me and the contributing writers whose letters are showcased in With Love.

Perhaps one of the primary overarching goals of With Love was to create a historical artifact that was by and for the queer Filipino American community to tell our story in our own words. I'm grateful to all of the contributing writers for not only their time in writing letters to their younger selves, but also their willingness to share vulnerable, honest, and encouraging pieces of their lives with readers. This book is a culmination of a huge community effort aimed to provide readers with valuable life lessons to pass on to present and future generations.

Time is precious. We are here for only a brief moment and then –*POOF* – history. So I encourage you to take the time needed to engage in this exercise of writing to your younger self. At first, it may feel incredibly difficult, but it will be well worth it. In doing so, I hope you are able to reflect on your growth, resilience, strength, and ways in which your story moves the community and the world forward.

With Love,
Dustin

REFERENCES

Almirol, E. B. (1982). Rights and obligations in Filipino American Families. *Journal of Comparative Family Studies*, *13*(3), 291–306. http://www.jstor.org/stable/41601309

Blair, S. L. (2014). Parental involvement and children's educational performance: A comparison of Filipino and U.S. Parents. *Journal of Comparative Family Studies*, *45*(3), 351–366. http://www.jstor.org/stable/24339542

Bureau, U. S. (2023). Census Bureau releases 2020 Census data for nearly 1,500 detailed race and ethnicity groups, tribes and villages. *Census. gov*. https://www.census.gov/newsroom/press-releases/2023/2020-census-detailed-dhc-file-a.html

Braun, K. L., & Nichols, R. (1997). Death and Dying in Four Asian American Cultures: A Descriptive Study. *Death Studies, 21*(4), 327–359. https://doi-org.norcocollege.idm.oclc.org/10.1080/074811897201877

Burnette, J. & Hardesty, P. (2018). *Adulting 101: #Wisdom4Life*. BroadStreet Publishing Group.

Cameron, J. (2022). *The artist's way: A spiritual path to higher creativity*. New York. TarcherPerigee.

David, E.J.R. (2013). *Brown skin, white minds: Filipino -/American postcolonial psychology*. Information Age Publishing, Inc.

Haim-Litevsky, D., Komemi, R., & Lipskaya-Velikovsky L. (2023). Sense of belonging, meaningful daily life participation, and well-being: Integrated Investigation. *International Journal of Environmental Research and Public Health, 20*(5). https://www.ncbi.nlm.nih.gov/pmc/articles/PMC10002207/

It Gets Better. (2024). Empowering LGBTQ+ youth to define their own journey. *It Gets Better.* Retrieved from https://itgetsbetter.org/

Jones, J. M. (2023). LGBT identification in U.S. ticks up to 7.1%. *Gallup.com.* Retrieved from https://news.gallup.com/poll/389792/lgbt-identification-ticks-up.aspx

Mohamed, B., & Rotolo, M. (2023). Christianity among Asian Americans. *Pew Research Center.* Retrieved from https://www.pewresearch.org/religion/2023/10/11/christianity-among-asian-americans/

Ocampo, A. C. (2016). *The Latinos of Asia: How Filipinos break the rules of race.* Stanford University Press.

Ocampo, A. C. (2023). *Brown and gay in LA: The lives of immigrant sons.* New York University Press.

Pew Research Center. (2012). Asian Americans: A mosaic of faith. *Pew Research Center.* Retrieved from https://www.pewresearch.org/religion/2012/07/19/asian-americans-a-mosaic-of-faiths-overview/

Simmons-Duffin, S. (2023). 'Life free and die?' The sad state of the U.S. life expectancy. *NPR.* Retrieved from https://www.npr.org/sections/health-shots/2023/03/25/1164819944

The Trevor Project. (2022). 2022 national survey on LGBTQ youth mental health. *The Trevor Project.* Retrieved from https://www.thetrevorproject.org/survey-2022/

The Trevor Project. (2023). 2023 U.S. national survey on mental health of LGBTQ young people. *The Trevor Project.* Retrieved from https://www.thetrevorproject.org/survey-2023/

Warikoo, N., Chin, M., Zillmer, N., & Luthar, S. (2020). The influence of parent expectations and parent-child relationships on mental health in Asian American and White American Families. *Sociological Forum, 35*(2), 275–296. https://www.jstor.org/stable/48586765

ACKNOWLEDGEMENTS

This work is a labor of love that I could not have ushered into existence alone and in a vacuum.

With the help of Dr. Pat Lindsay Catalla Buscaino (Dr. Pinky), this book became a reality. I met Dr. Pinky when I contributed my own creative writings and personal stories to her anthology, *The Kuwento Book*. In getting to know Dr. Pinky, she demystified the process of publishing a book. She was generous and kind in offering her time and energy to support me with resources via her publishing company Kuwento Co. Reader, without her, this book would not be sitting in your hands as a tangible artifact of our histories as queer Filipinos in America and abroad. Thank you, Dr. Pinky.

In my search for community member participation in this project, I collaborated with SoCal Filipinos (@socalfilipinos), a nonprofit organization that connects the Filipino community, particularly in Southern California, through sharing content, workshops, and events. Jason Lustina, one of the organization's co-founders, was a key connection I made in the last few years who truly helped advance this project, and its calls for submissions, in proportions I could not have imagined. Thanks to Jason and SoCal Filipinos for working with me to make announcements about this project to their Instagram audience, which at the time had more than 160,000 followers. Leaders, friends, and strangers near and far then spread the word on social media and through word of mouth. I am humbled by the magnitude of the call's reach.

I'd like to acknowledge and send thanks to Megan Dela Cruz. I've known Megan for about seven years. She is a colleague and dear friend. I admire her for challenging me on many occasions to use an ethnic studies lens to examine how I engage with the world. Megan was gracious enough to not only contribute a letter for this book, but to also provide feedback and support along the way. With her support, I felt comfortable knowing I was pushing myself to be a better writer and advocate for the queer Filipino community around the world.

Thank you to all 50 fellow queer Filipinos who contributed letters to With Love. I hope you found healing in the process of writing a letter to your younger selves. Without your willingness to share such deep and personal stories, there would be no book. Your thoughts and messages will resonate with readers for years to come.

And finally, I want to acknowledge and thank my partner, Jamal. I think the world of him and he thinks the world of me. Through his words and gestures, he consistently gives me the confidence and encouragement to show up authentically and fully even when it's hard. Working on this book was hard. Terrifying in fact. Committing myself to holding others' personal letters of hurting and healing in this project has been nerve-racking. Jamal has been my best friend and life companion who continues to remind me that I am equipped to do this work. With *his* love, I am able to bring you *With Love.*

CONTRIBUTING AUTHORS

AJ Johnson was raised on Graton Rancheria and Pomo land in what is known as California, had the privilege of playing basketball and studying on the land of the Kalapuya tribe at the University of Oregon, and is currently living on the unceded land of the Quandamooka people in Queensland, Australia. They describe themselves as a sensitive, biracial, non-binary neurodivergent weirdo who is blessed to be doing their life's work in promoting our collective healing from the trauma of living in a misogynistic, heteronormative, colonized, capitalist reality and being a nonjudgmental witness to others' journey through the sometimes harrowing, sometimes magical human experience.

Alyssa B.V. Cahoy earned a BA in Health Sciences and English from Rice University. The common thread connecting Alyssa's pursuits across disciplines is the centering of community. Alyssa's scholarship investigates how experiences of chronicity (illness, cultural amnesia, poetic tradition) are molded by a sociopolitical milieu. Her previous research works are community-engaged studies, including cancer prevention among Asian-American populations and sexual health promotion in minority-serving institutions. As a Pinay writer, her work focuses on Marxist-feminist criticism and postcolonial thought, experimenting with storytelling modes such as narrative, oral history, and digital photography.

Andre Zarate is a forever educator, edupreneur, and education leader from Mount Vernon, NY. He has taught middle school grades from Chicago, NY, Philadelphia, and DC. He is also a tennis enthusiast, writer, artist, and creative learning to incorporate all of himself into the educational space. He is currently creating a queer-centered space called "House of Legends," which centers the needs of queer of color youth by using imagination, art, and literacy to come back home to themselves. He's currently finishing his doctorate in education at the University of Pennsylvania Graduate School of Education centering his research on Filipinx Queer Youth and their use of imagination to make sense of their queer identities while defining queer joy. His current life motto is taken from Dr. Michael Sepidoza Campos's dissertation: "queer the mind, unfurl the body, open the heart."

AV "AudVision" is a non-binary Hip Hop Artist who was born and raised in Southeast San Diego. Many of their work is used to express the thoughts of gender, social issues, and personal stories. A goal in mind with AV's work is to be able to wholeheartedly express and connect with others who may feel similar to what is shown in the music they create.

Dr. Arnel Calvario Ripkens is the founder of UC Irvine's own Kaba Modern and Kaba Modern Legacy. He also served as the Board President of the international 501c3 non-profit dance organization, Culture Shock International from 2016-2023 and is currently an active member of the world-renowned dance crew "the KINJAZ." He has managed dance crews Kaba Modern, Fanny Pak, the Beat Freaks, & Kinjaz during their runs on MTV's hit show America's Best Dance Crew. Arnel also helped manage Kinjaz during their 2017 run on NBC's World of Dance. In collaboration with Culture Shock Los Angeles, he piloted a dance therapy program serving neurodivergent youth and currently works as a doctor of occupational therapy for the Long Beach Unified School District.

Blaine Valencia is queer and Filipinx from the suburbs of San Diego, California. The son of immigrants from Ilocos Sur and Bataan, he was raised with an ear for Ilocano, Tagalog, and Kapampangan, and a tongue soaked in *pinapaitan, lugaw, miki, and pinakbet*. Blaine is currently a practicing attorney based out of Los Angeles, California.

Brandon English is a Filipinx-American Multidisciplinary Artist located in Los Angeles, CA. He is an in-house Casting Director & Producer for Roundabout Entertainment. He has cast many projects for Disney+, Hulu, and Amazon Studios, such as Small & Mighty, Summer Time Rendering, and Love & Karma. Founder of Morenx Media, he is most known for his critically acclaimed short film "Bakla," which was screened at NewFilmmakers Los Angeles, Vancouver Queer Film Festival, CinemQ, and many more! He advocates strongly for Diverse & Representative Media, both in front and behind the camera.

Bryant de Venecia is an artist, organizer, and activist. He works in the labor movement representing healthcare workers across Hawaii as a union organizer with the Hawai'i Nurses' Association, OPEIU Local 50. Bryant is an immigrant from the Philippines and is a proud member of the LGBTQIA+ community. Outside of work, you can find him paddleboarding, volunteering at the local community health center, working on portraits, and acting in independent films and local theaters.

Bunny Anne (she/her) is a 23-year-old genderfluid, mainly feminine gender-identifying polyamorous pansexual Filipino-American born and raised by first generation immigrants in San Diego, California. She is interested in cultural, environmental, and linguistic anthropology. While spending time with her rats, dogs, and hamster, she also loves learning, homemaking, and exploring careers.

Dianara Rivera (she/her) is Director of Narrative Strategy at Asian American Resource Workshop by day, and essayist, poet, and dance enthusiast by night. She is Pilipina, Puerto Rican, and a lesbian, and has found and given immense care in communities of Pilipinx women, femmes, and non-men. As Director of Narrative Strategy, she leads storytelling projects that support AARW's organizing strategy. As a creative she explores all the ways she learned to be natural, and excavates all the little ways in the past she learned to take her own power.

Dominic I.J. is a first-generation, gay Filipino from Southern California (specifically Orange County). As of 2024, he is a graduate researcher at the University of California, Irvine pursuing a PhD in Biological Sciences with a focus on neuroimmunology, the intersection between the nervous system and the immune system. His current work investigates the impact of coronavirus infection on Alzheimer's Disease pathology within the brain. Dominic's experience as a queer Filipino scientist continues to inform his belief that personal identity and scientific identity are inseparable and more intertwined than traditional ideas of a "pure, unbiased" culture of science.

Lakan Guro elle Zulueta (they/them) is a Kali practitioner from New Jersey, who also works as a R/D chemist. They have been training Kali since September 2021, and teaches in their academy: Filipino Kali Academy in Norwood, NJ under the tutelage of Master Ace Ramirez and Guro Kris Ramirez. elle also plays video games and draws in their free time.

Francis Joseph J. Gallego is currently working as an Outpatient Oncology SW and has his own private psychotherapy practice. He has been actively involved in social justice since he was 17 and believes in the power of intersectionality and working on intergenerational trauma and healing. Francis has professional work experience working in both the East and West Coast, as well as on Oʻahu. He has experience working with communities of color, HIV/AIDS, Women, LBTQIA, and AAPI/API, as well as severely mentally ill populations providing intensive case management, DBT, and psychotherapy.

Gabe Sagisi graduated in 2019 from UC Davis and received his Bachelor's in Sociology, Organizational Studies with a minor in Technology Management. He currently works as an Associate Project Manager at the Institute for Healthcare Improvement (IHI), an organization in Boston that employs improvement science to advance and sustain better outcomes in health and healthcare across the world. He currently supports IHI's Europe work, Strategic Partnerships, and Faculty Operations. Prior to IHI, Gabe worked at the Asian & Pacific Islander American Health Forum (APIAHF) supporting Asian Americans, Native Hawaiians, and Pacific Islanders nationally to mitigate the impact of COVID-19 in their communities.

Gabriella Buba is a writer and chemical engineer who likes to keep explosive pyrophoric materials safely contained in pressure vessels, or between the covers of her books. She writes adult epic fantasy for bold, brown, bi women who deserve to be centered in stories. She has a novel SAINTS OF STORM AND SORROW released June of 2024 from Titan Books. She has a Filipino Fantasy short story in the anthology Strange Religion: Speculative Fiction of Spirituality, Belief, & Practice and short stories placed in Sci Phi Journal, PodCastle Fiction, and an essay on Filipino Identity and Language in Prairie Fire Press.

Grayson Villanueva (he/they) is a Filipino-American recording artist, music producer, film & TV session singer, and voice actor hailing from the vibrant city of Los Angeles. With a career spanning over a decade, Grayson has made a name for himself in the entertainment industry as a versatile and talented artist. He has lent his vocal talents to several high-profile projects, including voicing Tae Young in 4*TOWN from Disney Pixar's Turning Red, which earned him a Grammy nomination.

Grayson has had the privilege of working with some of the biggest names in the music industry, such as Billie Eilish, FINNEAS, Jordan Fisher, Josh Levi, Janelle Monáe, and Keala Settle. He has also built a strong reputation as an a cappella singer/beatboxer, performing with the current lineup of The House Jacks and Filosophy.

With his impressive skills and track record of success, Grayson is not only an accomplished artist but also a valuable mentor and teacher. He is passionate about creating open, collaborative spaces, sharing his knowledge and experience with others, and has become a sought-after coach and mentor for aspiring performers and producers alike.

Harlee Castro Balajadia is a First Generation Queer Filipino-America born and raised in Long Beach, CA. He is the Current Choral / Vocal / Music Appreciation Director at Charles Evas Hughes Middle School in Bixby Knolls. Outside of the classroom, he is a full-time vocalist and arts administrator for various organizations throughout the entire West Coast. He can be seen singing with The Filharmonic and Filosophy, Long Beach Camerata Singers, The Candlelight Carolers, and seen working with Choral Audacity, the Vocal Jazz Academy, and Voices for Social Justice. Harlee is grateful for Dustin to provide this platform to share his story.

Hazel Bondoc Carranza is a mental health advocate and content creator on Instagram and TikTok who created the character "Tita Celing" and skits called "Talk to Tita Advice Hotline" and "Tita's Translations." She grew up in Tondo, Manila, Philippines, and Southern California, but now lives in Canada. She shares a part of her story being a Filipino native who now lives in her second settlement country.

Jeff DeGuia is a writer and creative from Chicago, Illinois. He currently works at an Asian American serving social justice organization on their policy team. He's been living in California for 11 years and is still pursuing his dreams of storytelling and uplifting other POC LGBTQ+ creatives in the mainstream media. Prior to moving to California, at 19, he founded the nonprofit organization ManilaStar Events which aimed to create opportunities for Asian American artists and inspire youth to pursue their dreams in entertainment and creativity.

Jensen Reyes is a nonbinary Filipinx American interdisciplinary artist and co-author of the queer Filipino and woman-led poetry anthology "100 Pieces of Poetry by People Just Like You and Me." Residing in occupied Lenapehoking (New York City) they work during the day at a bakery but still write and create music in their free time. Having lived several lives, they've left pieces of their heart in occupied Tongva Los Angeles, Manila, Taipei, Seoul, Tokyo, and other places. You may find them on most SNS platforms @jensen_hari or by typing "Queer Asians" into Google image search (no, seriously).

Jessica Lustina Afable is a queer, second-generation Filipina-American born and raised in Tracy, California. Jessica adores her Illocano and Tagalog roots, and she is proud to be a Central Valley native. Jessica graduated with a degree in Biological Sciences with an emphasis in Human Biology and a minor in Interdisciplinary Public Health from the University of California, Merced. After graduating, Jessica worked in emergency medicine and will graduate from her Registered Nursing program in May 2024. She continues to advocate for equity and high-quality healthcare for underserved communities, especially the

LGBTQIA+ community. Most of all, she has always had a love for words, and writing holds a sincere part of her heart. Jessica is honored to share a piece of her life within this beautiful space amongst amazing storytellers.

Jobert E. Abueva is the author of *Boy Wander* – A Coming of Age Memoir (Rattling Good Yarns Press) and is the inaugural winner of the Lambda Literary J. Michael Samuel Prize for emerging LBTQ writers over 50. Also: Arch and Bruce Brown Foundation Literary Award for historical LGBTQ short fiction, Writer's Advice prize for flash memoir, two National Arts Club literary scholarships. Credits: The New York Times, The Philadelphia Inquirer, Beyond Queer Words, Harrington's Gay Men's Fiction Quarterly, Instinct Magazine, Poetry Nippon. Born in Manila, Jobert is a global marketer and resides in New Hope, Bucks County, PA. www.jobertabueva.net

Joel Baker is a 34-year-old pansexual cis male. He is mixed race, half White and half Filipino (mistiso). He is a second-generation Filipino-American. His dad is White and his mom is Filipino. He was born and raised in Chula Vista (San Diego), California. He is the black sheep of the family because he is an artist and a liberal. He is culturally Catholic but not actually. He has a large extended Filipino family unit of cousins and aunts and uncles and a grandma. So, even though his dad passed away when he was 16, all these people were there to help raise him, because that's how Filipinos are, always big tight-knit families.

Jonny Aliga is a third-year undergraduate student at UCLA. He was born and raised in Inglewood, California. Being one of the only Filipinos in his classes, it was hard for him to find a sense of community and identity, but this prepared him to face even more difficult situations later in life. He has a passion for food, so much so that he wants to work in the food manufacturing industry and someday create his beverage business that highlights calamansi.

JP Rogers is an award-winning pianist, producer, singer, and recording artist from Los Angeles, CA, and thrilled to share his story on With Love. An early love for the piano led him to formally study in college on a full scholarship. He has piano accompanied by LA Phil violinist Paul Stein, singer/actress Jennie Kwan (Avatar: The Last Airbender), and for singer/actress Nayah Damasen (Monster High: The Movie) on ToonGoggles' FanlalaTV. JP is a member of the vocal a cappella group Filosophy, an affiliate group created by The Filharmonic (NBC's The Sing-Off, Pitch Perfect 2, The Late Late Show), appearing on the album "Filled With Cheer" and its supporting music video "Go Tell It On The Mountain/Ain't No Mountain High Enough" and most recently on the group's newest EP "Profiles." As a fellow Fillie, JP has performed at Downtown Disney's LIVE! stage, LA City Hall, Universal Pictures' Violent Night movie screenings, hosted by AMC, the Long Beach Filipino Festival, and headlined Acapalooza 2023 in Las Vegas. JP is a featured background vocalist on the upcoming new album "Brazilian Project 2" by GRAMMY® nominated jazz ensemble Catina DeLuna & Lado B, and making the jump to the big screen next, with plans to star in a biopic about an up-and-coming DJ in New York City. JP enjoys taking drop-in acapella classes, attending local shows and conventions, exploring LA, and hiking with his Chihuahua Dachshund, Canelo. IG: @jpxrogers

Lani Fontillas, 33, First/Second generation Filipino American. Lani grew up in a Caucasian town, where she sought cultural acceptance. Her sexuality was her biggest secret, carrying it with guilt from a Catholic Filipino family.

LJ Balajadia is a young man living in Los Angeles County. He enjoys long walks on short beaches and short walks to the refrigerator. He imagines himself in another life as a bard who sings songs of fabulous heroes but in this life, he's trying to earn just enough money to feed himself and do what he loves.

Manny Garcia is a yoga teacher, movement coach, public speaker, and a founder/owner of The Collective Yoga Co-op in Chicago, IL. Manny's teaching path is dedicated to accessibility and inclusion. His studio, The Collective Yoga Co-op, opened in January 2023 and is dedicated to centering and uplifting LGBTQ+ teachers and teachers of color. When not teaching yoga, you can catch Manny at the dog beach with his pup Kaia, eating ice cream on a patio, or planning his next travel adventure.

Mara De La Rosa is an award-winning queer-POC writer and producer. She was the associate producer for the Ambies award-nominated podcast Navigating Narcissism at Red Table Talk Podcasts and iHeartMedia. Mara wrote, starred, and produced her latest short, Queerfully Departed, which raised over $20,000 through a fundraising campaign. She co-founded Queenfest LA, an International Women's Day variety show supporting women throughout Los Angeles. She was a Film Independent and Outfest Fellow. She also studied at The Groundlings and Upright Citizens Brigade theaters. Other films include BAES Welcome, BASTARD, The Outbreak, and I Like Femme Lesbians.

Mary Sabino is a mid-thirties pansexual Filipina who didn't come out until she was in her thirties. She is currently living her dream of working for one of the largest global sportswear companies in the world, a place where she credits finding the space to be her truest form of self.

Megan Dela Cruz is a disabled queer Pinay educator and community organizer based in the Inland Empire. She's passionate about creating accessible and sustainable communities of care. She's an Aquarius sun, a Cancer rising, and a Gemini moon.

Dr. Michelle Fortunado-Kewin (she/they) is a Filipino-American social worker in the San Francisco Bay Area. She works part-time as a school social worker and as an adjunct instructor/lecturer. Outside of work, she enjoys spending time with her dog and partner, hanging out at the beach, and visiting local coffee and boba shops.

MJ BH (he/him/his) is an aspiring musician and lover of all things food – cooking and consumption. He recently graduated with a Doctor of Psychology in Organizational Psychology, with goals of diving into the organizational system and finding ways to improve it for all. When he's not working on these goals, he spends his time in his music ministry and occasional trips to the gym (aka Disneyland/DCA). He shares his appreciation for this project to promote the importance of telling our stories for current and future generations to come.

Nicholas Pilapil is a Filipino American playwright. His plays have been presented nationwide, from the renowned Geffen Playhouse in Los Angeles to the Tony Award-winning Victory Gardens in Chicago and the legendary Samuel French Off Off Broadway Festival. His work is published by Samuel French, Smith & Kraus, and his collection of monologues, Other Monologues, is a winner of The Astringent Award and is published by Astringent Press. His critically acclaimed short film I Don't Love You (hailed by Philippine News as "laugh-out-loud funny") premiered at the Los Angeles Asian Pacific Film Festival and the Philippine International Film Festival.

O. Ayes is a queer Filipina writer who grew up in the Midwest. She has taught at universities in the Midwest and East Coast, as well as international schools in Tanzania, Indonesia, and The Netherlands. Her writing appears in TAYO Literary Magazine, Sukoon, The Nervous Breakdown, Blackbird, and elsewhere.

Patrick Anthony Asence-Arradaza is a 40-year-old gay man living in Anaheim, CA with his husband Richie and their Shiba Inu, Miso. He has seen a lot in his life and accomplished a lot but as the years have gone by, he has yet to fully define his life as a whole. He continues to live this life wholeheartedly and with love. The adventure continues and it is truly out there.

Paul Jochico is a multi-disciplinary teacher with training in dance, yoga and psychology. He was born and raised in New York (on Lenape land) and draws inspiration from the culture of his birth, the culture of his ancestors, and his journey of decolonization along the way. Writing is an evolution of his artistry and a re-membering of the power of storytelling to remind us that we are all connected as *kapwa*, shared inner-self.

P. M. is an immigrant, first-generation, queer Tagalog/Filipina/o/x/American appointed as assistant professor of Critical Race, Gender & Sexuality Studies at Cal Poly Humboldt. They teach classes in Asian/American Studies, transnational gender and sexuality studies, performance studies, media and cultural studies, and science and technology studies (STS). A multidisciplinary scholar, performer, and community advocate, their research interests coalesce in the study of mediated bodies in performance. Their current scholarship translates into multiple projects that amplify underserved Asian/American voices through ethnographic writing, drag performance art as Maria Art Susya Purisima Tolentino (Ma. Arte), and decolonial praxis in the classroom.

P.M. writes in Tagalog as a reflection of their own ethnolinguistic background as someone born in and who spent their childhood in Quezon City, Metro Manila, Philippines. They want to acknowledge the privilege of Tagalog's global circulation as a national symbol of a state, a republic, and encourage us to embrace not only the ethnolinguistic diversity of peoples from the Philippines but all of the hybrids that emerge and disappear through use.

P.M. shares their gratitude to Jose Mari Cuartero, Monica FA Wong Santos, Oscar Tantoco Serquiña Jr., and Madilene B. Landicho for reviewing their writing in Tagalog. The final iteration of the Tagalog letter, *Wag Ka Nang Malungkot*, reflects their collective ideas and revisions. The final translation of the letter was written by P.M. To hear a reading of *Wag Ka Nang Malungkot* in Tagalog, visit: https://youtu.be/UZHtcwKKbZ8

Ramon Alcantara is an educator based in Southern California. They are a multidisciplinary storyteller and aspire to give back to the community through art and advocacy. Ramon is committed to mentorship, especially for young Filipinos across industries. They provide consultation to aspiring graduate students and those new to their respective careers.

Rana Rosanes was born in the Philippines and migrated to America when she was only five years old. She graduated with a Bachelor's Degree in Women's Studies and a minor in English from San Diego State University way back in 2011. She enjoys watching sports (basketball & football mostly), Yelping new places (long-running Yelp Elite), Disney & all its subsidiaries, and enjoys the occasional drink or two. Most of all, Rana loves spending time with her bff turned gf, Val, her parents (Roel & Royina), and her younger sibling, Riane.

Shout out to you four, my reasons & my solace.

Resi Ibañez is a poet and storyteller originally from the northern New Jersey / New York City area and is now based in Massachusetts. They have been previously published in community projects such as Outside the XY: Queer, Black, and Brown Masculinity by bklyn boihood, Powerful Asian Moms by Spill Stories, and They Rise Like a Wave: an Anthology of Asian American Women Poets by Blue Oak Press. Their writing has been supported by the Pioneer Valley Writers Workshop and Tin House, and they have performed as a featured poet with MassPoetry and the Emily Dickinson Museum. They are currently working on their first full-length poetry collection.

Ron Blakely (they/them) is a Southern California-based singer, songwriter, actor, and recording artist of Black and Filipino heritage. With a passion for music from a young age, Ron participated in school talent shows, church bands, and karaoke competitions before studying voice and guitar in high school and college. Influenced by soul, R&B, folk, musical theatre, and pop, Ron has an eclectic range of musical pursuits and aims to continue creating work that speaks to many walks of life. Ron is currently working on their independently released debut solo LP entitled "Blue" that released in Spring 2024.

Ryan Dalusag, LCSW is a second-generation, queer cis-male Filipino-American residing in Orange County, California. He works as a Licensed Clinical Social Worker and is the owner of Well-Being Heritage Therapeutic Services, a mental health therapy practice dedicated towards supporting Asian-American/Pacific Islander adults who struggle with issues like anxiety, trauma, and identity. In his free time, he enjoys spending time with friends, trying new foods, traveling, and playing games.

Sam C. Tenorio was born and raised in Southern California, but now proudly resides in West Philadelphia. He is an Assistant Professor of Women's, Gender, and Sexuality Studies and African American Studies at Penn State University, whose work is primarily concerned with questions of political dissent, carcerality, antiblackness, and trans and gender non-conforming life.

Sean-Joseph Takeo Kahāokalani Choo is a multi-ethnic + multi-hyphenate theater artist and composer from Honolulu, and the Lead Steward + Head Jester of Kamamo House, a queer-centered theatre, artist cultivation/advocacy organization, and podcast. He has worked with Honolulu Theatre for Youth, Kumu Kahua Theatre, Hawaii Shakespeare Festival, Atlantic For Kids, and TheaterWorks USA, to name a few. Sean was honored to be a 2021 Creative Lab Hawai'i Playwrights Immersive Program Fellow, with mentor Chay Yew.

He was also delighted to be one of The Playwrights Realm's inaugural Native American Artist Lab members, mentored by Rhiana Yazzie and Victoria Nalani Kneubuhl.

tiano p. is a queer second-generation Filipino American who was born and raised in Illinois before bopping around the U.S. to explore himself, his sexuality, his Filipino-ness, and places he can call community. tiano writes with hopes to expand his individual and our collective capacities to experience our wholeness as people.

Timothy A.M. Tumbokon was born and raised in a small town in New Jersey. Timothy currently has a Master's degree in International Relations. Now he is working on becoming a writer and filmmaker along with conserving Filipino Art and culture.

Toby Javier is a vocalist and actor based in Los Angeles. He is originally from Metro Manila, Philippines. He has performed for the nation's premiere Asian American theatre company, East West Players. He has acted in numerous network television shows and film projects. Alongside pursuing acting, Toby is developing his work in music through singing with various groups, providing vocals for multimedia projects, and debuting his solo cabaret show.

TR Deanon (they/them) navigates this life with the curiosity of a 6-year-old and a nonchalant don't-give-a-f*ck attitude like a 90-year-old. If it doesn't bring them joy, it's a no for them. To stay grounded and at peace, they practice yoga, write, get lost in stories, and go on 2-mile walks with their dogs in nature. For funsies, they like to pretend they're so much better on rollerskates than they really are. Because they can't sit still – thanks to their neurodivergence – home is wherever they are with their two dogs, exploring all parts of the world.

Vanessa Aczon was born and raised in the San Francisco Bay Area, California, whose ancestral roots stem from Ilocos Norte, Philippines. When not immersed in work, she indulges in her passion for dancing, venturing into uncharted streets and paths alongside her pup and loved ones, and finding solace in coffee shops and bookstores. Vanessa is intrigued by her family's inherited wisdom and captivated by Filipino mythology and pre-colonial teachings.

Warjay Naigan (they/them) is a 28-year-old queer disabled AuDHD (Autistic + ADHD) FilAm living in Southern California. They are a community organizer, friend, sibling, student, cat parent, gamer, musician, and so much more. Their life experiences have informed their dream of radical liberation for all oppressed peoples.

ABOUT THE AUTHOR

DR. DUSTIN E. DOMINGO is a writer, singer, performer, voice actor, podcaster, producer, educator and trier of new things. Based in Southern California, Dustin is a multidisciplinary creative and educator, dedicated to documenting histories and telling stories, especially those representing marginalized communities. Dustin holds a doctorate in organizational leadership and regularly seeks practical and artistic applications of his academic research, which explores diversity and cultural competence in shared spaces. His work has been published in various academic journals, books, and blogs. He produced for podcasts, including: *MeSearch*; *The Stories We're Proud to Share*; *HAVE YOU MET...*; and *Let's Circle Back*. His insights as a gay Filipino American man are featured in *GAMChat Podcast*; *Insufferable Academics*; and *Kuwento Co.* As a musician, Dustin was a founding member of Not So Sharp A cappella at UC Riverside, and a lead singer for Orange County based, #FOURTY4B. With #FOURTY4B, he released two albums: *FOURTY4B* and *From Us*. He is a singer for award winning group, Top Shelf Vocal, based in Los Angeles. With Filosophy, a subgroup of the Filharmonic composed of Asian American singers, Dustin is a regular live performer with credits at the Festival of Philippine Arts & Culture, Knott's Berry Farm, Disney's California Adventure, and Downtown Disney. His original songs, *Leap*, *Simple*, and *Lonely Mind* are featured tracks in discography by Norco Music. Other highlights include Dustin's contributions as content and outreach coordinator for BakitWhy.com, an online community which sought to represent the diversity of the Filipino American lifestyle; as well as his leadership role of Director of Curriculum for Lakas Mentorship, a program where Filipino American youths may find a sense of belonging and develop their ethnic identity. Learn more at www.dustindomingo.com.

ABOUT THE PUBLISHER

KUWENTO CO. is a writing, storytelling, and publishing company that empowers people to become authors who write, tell, and publish their *kuwentos,* pronounced *kwen-toh,* the Filipino word for story, narrative, or tale. We help you express your authentic self, provide a space to be heard, inspire others to do the same, and pass down your legacy to the next generation. Become an author today!

BOOKS PUBLISHED BY KUWENTO CO.
The Roots
The Oscar Tree
Bakas Ng Aking Buhay: Footprints of My Life
Living An Inspired Life: Dula Ng Aking Buhay
Salaysay Ng Aking Buhay: The Story of My Life
Chasing A Dream: A Beautiful, Heartfelt Story
The Kuwento Book: An Anthology of Filipino Stories + Poems
With Love: What We Wish We Knew About Being Queer And Filipino in America

www.KuwentoCo.com | info@kuwentoco.com | Follow @KuwentoCo

www.ingramcontent.com/pod-product-compliance
Lightning Source LLC
Chambersburg PA
CBHW021141090426
42740CB00008B/882